FRANCIS AND THÉRÈSE
GREAT 'LITTLE' SAINTS

Dedication

With love and gratitude to

Betty and Bryan
Christine and Andrew
Albert and Jan

and

In loving memory of

Sister Maria Mahon FSM

and

Father Joseph Doino OFM

FRANCIS AND THÉRÈSE
GREAT 'LITTLE' SAINTS

PATRICIA JORDAN FSM

GRACEWING

First published in 2012
by
Gracewing
2, Southern Avenue
Leominster
Herefordshire HR6 0QF
www.gracewing.co.uk

ISBN 978 085244 797 0

Typeset by Gracewing

Cover design by Bernardita Peña Hurtado

Contents

Contents

Foreword

Francis and Thérèse—two saints, a man and a woman separated by centuries, class, culture, who have had an unprecedented influence on the Church and indeed, in some way, on the whole of humanity. Their appeal transcends denominational and even faith boundaries, because they show us the best that our human nature is capable of. They are truly one of us —limited individuals belonging to a certain time and place, yet modelling for us the fullness of life that is a result of surrendering to God all that we have and are within the limits of our own era, and our own unique personality and giftedness. People such as Francis and Thérèse reflect our deepest desires for wholeness, freedom and peace. And Sr Patricia Jordan has placed them together in this study in order to help each one of us draw from their example what it means to be a person of love and littleness within our own sphere, as they were in theirs. Those who already know and love Francis will discover in St Thérèse one who reflects the same joy and simplicity as the saint of Assisi. Those who are devoted to Thérèse will find that Francis too is one of those 'little souls' who go straight to the heart of God in confidence and trust. While those who already love both saints will find them juxtaposed in one book which enriches our knowledge of the two of them as kindred spirits and soul friends.

I remember well my own first visit to Assisi. We travelled first through the Rieti Valley, stopping at the many small sanctuaries made holy by Francis's prayer and preaching: Greccio, the site of the first Christmas crib, Poggio Bustoni where had received confirmation of forgiveness, Fonte Colombo where he had written his Rule. These small churches and cloisters high among the mountains, with their vistas over the valley below, brought home not only the miles Francis had walked, but the remoteness of the places he had sought out for prayer in the midst of unsurpassed natural beauty. In Assisi itself the grand basilica had its own charm, but did not reflect Francis for me so much as the smaller churches and hermitages which dotted the landscape, bringing to mind his love for what was poor, hidden and close to nature. I found my own heart opening out in praise, with a sense of freedom and joy that suddenly touched my own creativity in unexpected ways. The Crucifix which had once spoken to Francis challenged me too to ask 'Lord, what do You want me to do?' and to take the next step with confidence.

Lisieux was different. Here the limitedness of Thérèse's world struck me immediately. One could walk from her family home to the cathedral where she had worshipped as a child, to the place where she had been at school with the Benedictine nuns, to the local Carmel which she had entered at the age of fifteen. A constrained ambience, a life limited like so many lives to one locality. Thérèse too loved the natural creation, but her contact with nature was not the craggy peaks and dark forests of Assisi. It was the gentle flowering meadows of Normandy, the river where her father had gone fishing, seaside towns not far away. Mostly Thérèse found God in the simple things: a small white flower, a hen gathering her chicks beneath her wings, the austere plainness of the Carmelite convent. Here in Lisieux holiness seemed close and accessible. It was the holiness of the ordinary person, and it was people such as these who first recognised the true holiness of

Thérèse and her 'Little Way', enabling them to grow close to a God who loves us unconditionally in all our weakness and neediness. When the relics of Thérèse came to this country I felt that many who journeyed far to venerate them were celebrating their own poor, ordinary lives and their own possibility of making a real difference through seemingly small acts of love and kindness.

What is the enduring appeal of these two saints who can seem so different and yet so alike? Surely it is their ability to cut through all the inessentials that we can falsely associate with holiness: severe mortification, grades of prayer, mystical experiences, theological knowledge and so forth, and instead go straight to the heart of the Gospel.

Each lives in a time when the Church and the world needed to hear the specific message they brought. The Church in Francis's time was enmeshed in a feudal system that emphasised hierarchy, power, control, and wealth. There seemed to be little room for the witness of poverty, little attention paid to the outcasts of society such as lepers, paupers, the displaced and marginalised. It was Francis's genius to show that a return to Gospel values was possible. That one lived with surrender and joy, witnessing to the life of Jesus among the poor, spreading the message by word and example, had immense power. The way of life he planned for the brothers who joined him was simple, imitable, an alternation of intense apostolic activity with periods of withdrawal for uninterrupted prayer. Francis's life affected everyone who came in contact with him, influencing not only his own brothers and Clare's sisters, but many other men and women in all walks of life, enabling them to share his charism of simplicity, peace, praise, community, and the service of the least. Francis did not criticise the Church. He just showed that there was another way to be Christian. And people recognised the truth of his message because he lived it out so joyfully and simply. He became the 'Christ of Umbria' eventually marked by the stigmata, a living image of his crucified Lord.

By contrast, in Thérèse's day the Church had become a fortress enmeshed in numerous rules and laws, marked by a mentality of rewards and punishments according to one's behaviour. The Church of the nineteenth century was in a position of reaction to anything secular. It was tainted by a Jansenitic spirit that made holiness inaccessible. One had to be at least a priest or a nun to even get onto the radar at all! Respectability was everything. Of course, many people did manage to see beyond these restrictions, but it took a Thérèse to remind us by her life and teaching that God is not a hard taskmaster, and that holiness is not about 'being perfect'. Holiness is union with God and, in Jesus, God is accessible to us all, no matter our individual circumstances. Again, like Francis, Thérèse did not criticise, instead she set out to discover and live the truth of what it means to love God and be loved in return. It was simple. It was nothing other than a joyful and confident abandonment to life. Our picture of God will influence how we relate to Him. Thérèse shows us a God who is human, close, and who loves us totally in our weakness and uniqueness.

Francis and Thérèse have a universal appeal because they just went straight to the gospel. They did not judge others. They just accepted responsibility for their own lives and pursued the truth as it was revealed to them step by step. These were not saints who wrote about degrees of prayer, climbing a mountain, the intricacies of canon law and multiple states and grades of perfection. They lived out their calling in love and service keeping their eyes on Jesus. 'It is confidence and confidence alone that leads to love' wrote Thérèse. This is what gave her the courage to step out and 'take Jesus by the heart'. If we are loved then what can hold us back? The greatest gift we can give another is our complete trust. It is all that is asked of us.

'My God and my All' was the constant prayer of Francis; while Thérèse wrote that 'To love is to give everything, it's to give oneself.' This gift of self was primary in the spirituality of Francis and Thérèse, each in their own way, and contemporaries recognised in them the power of that gift. Fear closes us up, only love enables us to fly. Sr Patricia Jordan shows how the great mendicant devotions of crib, cross and Eucharist can enable us too to find our wings and grow in love for the human Jesus, our friend and teacher.

Along the way Francis initiated a new form of life that broke with the old monastic stereotype and devised a way of living like Jesus and the apostles, close to God as a loving Father, and close to people, especially the poor and marginalised, who were also God's beloved children. Thérèse in her turn discovered a 'Little Way' that cuts through myriad rules and regulations and goes straight to God's heart. She challenges us to embark on the adventure of a love that can change the world through small things, small actions that are ultimately great because of the love that motivates them.

Both saints became images of Christ in their own way: Francis through the stigmata, Thérèse through her changing face; so that Ida Gorres can write of students, looking at a photo of Thérèse in her last illness, saying 'She looks like a female Christ.' We become like those we love, being changed even in our bodily being to resemble the beloved.

Both our saints lived with a song in their hearts and on their lips. Thérèse said that her life was a song celebrating God's merciful love. Francis in his turn was a troubadour, the first to write a poem, his 'Canticle of the Creatures', in the Umbrian dialect. Through both lives flows the music of transparency, joy, simplicity, closeness to the human Christ in love and minority or littleness. In this book we have the opportunity to learn more of their secret and sing the song that is our own life, breathed into us by the same Spirit of Love that animated Francis and Thérèse, if only we are open to listen and respond.

Elizabeth Ruth Obbard CJN

Preface

God, the Almighty, chose for himself as the place
of his appearance what was the very smallest and
most insignificant, a wretched stable in Bethlehem.

W hen asked to comment on this, Joseph Car-
dinal Ratzinger commented: '…it is a fact
that the choice of "little things" and "little
people" is characteristic of God's dealings with
humanity. We see this characteristic first of all in the
fact that God chooses the earth as his theatre of action,
this grain of dust in the universe; and in the fact that
there is Israel, a virtually powerless people, becomes
the vehicle for his own action; and again in the fact that
a completely unknown village, Nazareth, becomes his
home; finally, in the fact that the Son of God is born at
Bethlehem, outside the village in a stable. All of this is
consistent' (*God and the World*, p. 213).

Francis and Thérèse Great 'Little' Saints expresses how
this 'characteristic of God's dealings' with men and
women is at the heart of the spiritual life of Francis of
Assisi and Thérèse of Lisieux. If Baptism plunges us
into the Paschal Mystery of Christ, this man of the
thirteenth century and this woman of the nineteenth
expressed its energy of dying to self and rising to life in
Christ through a path of littleness. The Poverello, 'Little
Poor One', wanted his brothers and sisters to live
among their peers by a comparative adjective minor
(lesser) that would challenge them always to be the
least. Centuries later Thérèse recognized herself as a

'little flower' and described her journey of the spiritual life as the *petite voie* (little way). Both chose that same characteristic of God's dealing with our humanity to deal with his divinity.

The pursuit of growing in an awareness of being little, of focusing on the little people, the little things, and the little actions of daily life! The challenge of being lesser before others as we are before God! Such is the energy of Francis and Thérèse that needs to be revitalized that the hands of those of us in the twenty-first century may join theirs in making the world a new Bethlehem.

Regis J. Armstrong, OFM Cap
The John C. and Gertrude P. Hubbard Professor of
Religious Studies
The Catholic University of America
Washington, DC

Acknowledgements

At the end of leading a week's retreat, one of the Directors of the Retreat Centre gave a vote of thanks. Having worked as a missionary sister in remote areas, she said she was familiar with the saying: 'It takes a village to raise a child'. She then remarked that it takes a Minoress community to give a retreat and she thanked us for our witness as sisters. Although I led the retreat, my sisters were present giving support with liturgy preparation, music, power-point presentations and many practical matters that such a week involves. I now acknowledge that it takes a community to write a book! I say this because my sisters have given me time, space, support and encouragement throughout this project. I thank each one.

I am also indebted to Sr Elizabeth Ruth Obbard, solitary and author, for her unfailing guidance, encouragement and meticulous proofreading of my manuscript.

Sr Elizabeth has lived experience and knowledge of both the Carmelite and Franciscan way of life and this has enabled her to read with keen insight and offer valuable advice. Her illustrations have also enhanced this study on Francis and Thérèse.

Father Regis Armstrong, a renowned Franciscan scholar, very kindly read my work and wrote the Preface. Knowing something of his very busy schedule, I am deeply grateful and appreciative of his generous gift of time given to this project.

I wish to express my sincere gratitude to Tom Longford and to Rev Dr Paul Haffner, from Gracewing Publishing, for patient and detailed guidance in bringing the text to its present book form.

Finally, I wish to thank the owners of copyright material for their permission to reproduce extracts from the following: *Francis of Assisi, Early Documents*, vols 1,2, The Continuum International Publishing Group Ltd., New City; *Story of a Soul The Autobiography of St. Thérèse of Lisieux*, Translated by John Clarke, O.C.D. 1975, 1976, 1996 by Washington Province of Discalced Carmelites, ICS Publications, 2131 Lincoln Road, N.E. Washington, DC 20002-1199 USA; www.icspublications.org.

Introduction

Francis and Thérèse: Holding Hands Across the Centuries

In a curious way, the Poor Man of Assisi and the young nun of Lisieux stretch out hands to one another across the centuries, as if they were two children playing a children's game together.

Ronald Knox, *Lisieux and Assisi* (1936)

Why another book on two Saints whose lives have been written more times than any other Saints in the history of the Church? Because as far as I know, never before has a book attempted to portray Francis and Thérèse as kindred spirits, which is the aim of this book. Though separated by time, gender, country and culture they are united in the timeless and universal Gospel values of love and littleness. These characteristics have captivated the hearts of people of all ages, creeds and cultures in every century since their lives graced our earth.

While stressing love and littleness, we will travel with Francis and Thérèse through the down-to-earth lived experience of the human condition involving poverty, humility and patient suffering. These are part and parcel of the life of every person born within the limitations of a contingent human being. That Francis and Thérèse transformed these inevitable and unavoidable human experiences through love and littleness points to their genius and relevance for every one.

This approach is rooted in the Incarnation of Jesus Christ, God made man for us. He is our Way our Truth and our Life and, when taken seriously and radically, the life of the Son of God in human flesh and blood will shine through the humanity of our two beloved saints. They will serve as models and examples for us on the journey to God and they will challenge us in a way that is truly ordinary in an extraordinary way.

Chapter One will serve as an introduction to the lives of Francis and Thérèse. We will not give a detailed account as this can be found in the numerous books that are available but we will give enough information to paint their portraits in word and example.

Chapter Two will take us into the realm of love revealed in the God made flesh in Jesus Christ. We will root Francis and Thérèse in a Gospel spirituality that marks their lives and universal message. Their love of Scripture was the foundation of all they said and did. This love of the word of God led them to embrace and emulate the Word made flesh in Jesus Christ and they did this each in their own unique and God-given way. Strikingly, our two Saints focus particularly on three key events in the life of Jesus Christ: the crib, the cross and the Eucharist. As each had a tender love for Mary the Mother of Christ, evidence of this will weave through the text as appropriate.

Chapter Three will focus on one of these key points as Francis and Thérèse experienced them, namely the humble birth of the Son of God in the poverty of Bethlehem. Francis and Greccio, Thérèse and the Infant Jesus: we will demonstrate how Francis and Thérèse lived this mystery and the challenges it presents to every follower of the Incarnate Son of God.

Chapter Four will move us into the mystery of the cross and the way in which Francis and Thérèse understood and embraced this mystery in their own lives. Just as suffering is inherent in the human condition, so too, suffering, both interior and exterior, marked the lives of Francis and Thérèse. The consequences of the La Verna experience for Francis, and the devotion to the Holy Face for Thérèse, reveal the depth of their union with the Suffering Servant and the implications for every baptised follower of Christ.

Continuing the theme of love and littleness, Chapter Five leads us to a consideration of the Holy Eucharist, the mystery *par excellence* of humble, incarnate love and littleness. We will explore the depth of love and understanding that Francis and Thérèse had for the Holy Eucharist.

Chapter Six focuses on the primacy of love. This will be explored in the context of the extravagant love in the heart of God, reflected and expressed in love's response in the hearts of Francis and Thérèse.

Chapter Seven explores love and littleness as it was lived by Francis as a lesser brother, bringing to birth his charism and lasting legacy of minority. Thérèse too lived in love and littleness and gifted the Church and the world with her charism, which is expressed in her Little Way of Spiritual Childhood. Francis and Thérèse are truly kindred spirits and their Gospel message lives on. Both Saints continue to attract followers who walk the Gospel path of love and littleness in the uniqueness of their God-given call to fullness of life in Christ.

This little book has been in my heart for more than twenty years. As a MA student at The Franciscan Institute, St Bonaventure University, I completed a class assignment for the late Father Joseph Doino, OFM., a deeply spiritual man and an inspiring teacher. My topic was a comparative study of the spirituality of Francis and Thérèse. Because of my own love for Francis and Thérèse and the positive response and encouragement I received from Father Joe, I knew that the seed sown that day in my heart would one day bear fruit in a fuller exploration which I now present in this book. In writing it, I *know* I have been on a journey. I pray that as you read these pages, you too will have a similar experience.

Patricia Jordan FSM
Feast of The Annunciation 2012

Chapter One

Introducing Francis and Thérèse

Saints never grow old. They never become figures of the past, men and women of 'yesterday'. On the contrary, they are always men and women of the future, witnesses of the world to come.

Pope John Paul II, *Address in Lisieux* (1980).

Francis of Assisi

F rancis of Assisi is one of the best-known and universally loved saints in the Christian calendar. Born in 1182 in the ancient Roman city of Assisi, Francis was the welcome first child of Pietro Bernardone and his wife, Pica. Many legends surround his birth. We will recall only some of the relevant facts pertinent to this study and reflection.

Times of transition are problematic and the Assisi into which Francis was born was turbulent and changing. In many respects the twenty first century is similar to the thirteenth century and this becomes evident as the book unfolds. His immediate environment shaped Francis in much the same way as our environment shapes us today. This may serve as both a challenge and an incentive as we reflect on the relevance of a thirteenth century saint for our times.

Assisi was changing within the political, social and religious spheres. As Pope and Emperor fought for control of the City States, politics and religion shaped the character of the society into which Francis was born. Economic expansion and social change brought new challenges and possibilities. Alternative value systems created new problems and in Assisi these were manifest in the desire for power and control, wealth and possessions, status and self-glory.

Upward mobility motivated personal and communal decisions and inevitably some were left behind in the changing economic and social patterns that emerged. The rich became richer and more influential while the poor became even more marginalized than before. Does this sound familiar? Even more pertinent in a changing society is the place given or not given, to God, the Creator and giver of all good gifts. This was the Assisi of Francis's day which remains pertinent in our own twenty-first century. The way Francis struggled with the values in which he was immersed was for him, as it is for each one of us, the challenge of the Gospel. Holiness is not divorced from the everyday world in which we find ourselves; it is in fact the way in which we travel our own unique path to sainthood.

Prayer, reflection and wisdom are needed to look critically and sensitively at the times we live in, whether the thirteenth or twenty first century. To recognize and name the underlying structures and ideas that become the controlling symbols of our lives and read these signs in the light of the Gospel is a perennial challenge. It was for Francis in the thirteenth century and it is for us now.

In the thirteenth century, turmoil and confusion abounded in both Church and State and Francis was caught up in the cultural and religious upheaval sweeping across Europe. Conflict between the old and the new was keenly felt within the city of Assisi and in the heart of the young Francis. Shaped as he was by his wealthy, merchant background, Francis also aspired to the courtly life of chivalry and knighthood. The rising, rich merchant class aspired to the privileges held by the nobility. We often hear the saying 'money talks'. It did then and it does now.

So, as son of a rich merchant, Francis of Assisi enjoyed the life that wealth provides: social prestige, peer group status, ambitious dreams and all the pomp and popularity that surround such a lifestyle. It seemed to work for a time. Then something changed. Was it as sudden as the books about Francis seem to recall? Or was it a more gradual though less obvious working of divine grace in the heart of Francis?

Later in this chapter we will look briefly at a few key moments in the story of Francis that shaped his journey and paved the way for future generations. Without doubt his legacy is captured in the name he chose for himself and his followers: friars minor—little (lesser) brothers. Fraternity and littleness. How did Francis arrive at this sense of call and identity? This is what we will try to discover as we ponder on his life, his message, his mission and its relevance for us today. And we will compare this with the life, message, mission and relevance of St Thérèse of Lisieux. Before we look at the significant stages in the lives of these two great saints, let me introduce you to Thérèse and situate her too within her own time and place.

Thérèse of Lisieux

Like St Francis before her, St Thérèse of Lisieux is also one of the best-known and universally loved saints in the Christian calendar. Thérèse made her appearance in this world on 2 January 1873 in the small family house on Rue Saint-Blaise in the French town of Alençon. This is how her mother, Zelie Martin described the event. 'My little daughter was born yesterday, Thursday, at 11.30 at night. She is very strong and very well ... She seems to be very pretty. I am very happy ... She will be baptised tomorrow, Saturday'.[1] She was named Marie-Francoise-Thérèse on the 3 January 1873.

Thérèse was the ninth and last child in the Martin family. Prior to the birth of Thérèse, her parents, Louis and Zelie, had lost four children in infancy, therefore Thérèse was especially welcomed as a strong and healthy child. Unfortunately their joy and optimism were short-lived. Within two weeks Thérèse became seriously ill and unable to take her mother's milk. As Thérèse's condition worsened, her mother sought help from Rose Taille who managed to breast feed the little Thérèse and restore her health and strength. However the price was high for both baby and parents. Thérèse had to leave the security of the family home and loving, doting parents and remain with Rose who lived six miles away in Alençon. But Thérèse was happy with Rose and loved the countryside and within a year she was strong enough to return to her loving family.

Like the thirteenth century of St Francis's time, Alençon in the nineteenth century experienced turmoil and confusion in both the Church and the State. The Martin family had housed no less than nine soldiers during the Franco-Prussian war as conflict raged in the region of Alençon. Though the region had been liberated the people were fearful and worried in case another revolution would break out. Fear of political and religious conflict brought people to their knees. In May 1872 it is recorded that twenty thousand men, including Louis Martin, the father of Thérèse, made a pilgrimage to Chartres Cathedral. In the year of Thérèse's birth, prayers were being offered for the liberation of Pope Pius IX, a prisoner in Italy.[2] In the same year thirty thousand people made a pilgrimage to the Cathedral of Paray-le-Monial demanding that France be consecrated to the Sacred Heart of Jesus. This was not just a pious desire. It had political overtones in that the Catholics of France 'began to dream of a three-fold restoration: of the monarchy, of the Pope at the head of his states, and of the faith in the country'.[3] Politics and religion were closely entwined and then as now they are not always happy bedfellows!

Like Francis of Assisi, Thérèse belonged to a reasonably wealthy family. Both parents had successful businesses and the family could be described as the rising middle class of their day. Thérèse, like Francis, was shaped and influenced by the religious, political and social currents of her time, yet with amazing courage and creativity neither Francis nor Thérèse was bound by these in later years. Faith, God's call, and response to personal vocation, all contributed to the creative genius, originality and uniqueness that radiates from Assisi and Lisieux.

Both Francis and Thérèse perceived their call and identity in the same way that most of us grow and mature. They lived life with all its ups and downs, its joys and sorrows, its changes and challenges, within the context of family, friends, society, culture and the religious, political and social situation into which they were born. Yet within the seeming ordinariness of life, there is a mysterious freely given grace at work in every individual that is precious, unique and unrepeatable: pure gift. The great theologian, Hans Urs von Balthasar describes it as 'secreted in God, this 'individual law' freely promulgated ... by the pure grace of God'.[4]

Francis and Thérèse: The Early Years

Traditions and stories abound that suggest a divine predilection for Francis and Thérèse. The birth of Francis is sometimes set within legends suggesting details similar to the birth of Christ. His mother, Pica, prophesied that Francis would be one of the best of men and his merits would make of him a son of God. Naming him Giovanni, after St John the Baptist, was for Pica a significant gesture. Following the biblical tradition of naming as a revelation of identity, mission and destiny, Pica's choice of baptismal name for her son placed him in that special category of being a great preacher, a herald of the Great King. In later life, Francis described himself in these very terms: 'a herald of the great King'.[5]

The name Giovanni did not last long. Pietro Bernardone, Francis's father was less smitten by the name Giovanni and decided to call his son Francesco, meaning 'Frenchman' or 'Little Frenchy'. It is thought that the reason for the change of name was influenced by Pietro's travels to France where he purchased fine fabrics that increased his wealth and status as a cloth merchant. Therefore the name Francesco was more in keeping with the destiny Pietro envisaged for his son in both wealth and nobility.

The naming of Thérèse was also carefully chosen. Marie-Francoise-Thérèse. Invoking the patronage of Our Blessed Lady and the gentle St Francis de Sales, Thérèse's special patron was the great St Teresa of Avila. Unlike the Bernardone family, both parents approved and nurtured the God-given destiny of their newborn. Significantly, Thérèse would eventually follow in the footsteps of the great St Teresa. Significant too was the fact that Zelie, Thérèse's mother was a member of the Third Order of St Francis of Assisi, and undoubtedly Thérèse would have imbibed the Franciscan spirit that pervaded the family home, close as it was to the Poor Clare Convent that her sister Leonie would eventually enter for a time.

Francis and Thérèse: Childhood and Adolescence

We know that Francis was his mother's favourite son and love and care was lavished on him in the family home. It was a home of plenty and Francis lived a reasonably easy life similar to many of the rich nobility. Pica was a devout and pious woman and she nurtured Francis's faith and devotion just as surely as she believed in his call to greatness like his baptismal patron, John the Baptist. In time Francis was sent to St George's school where he had a basic education but never made a name for himself as an academic. No, he was more interested in knights and chivalry—just like the patron of his school, St George. The dream had begun!

We could say that Thérèse was home-schooled for the first years of her life. The tragic death of her mother when Thérèse was four years of age deeply affected the little girl and it was followed by a move to Lisieux to be closer to other relatives. Bereavement brings its own pain and turmoil within a close-knit family and once again Thérèse experienced a separation that some describe as abandonment. Two separations in the space of four years was a shattering experience for Thérèse and she would remember the effect this had on her young life. Let us listen to her own words:

> I must admit, Mother, my happy disposition completely changed after Mamma's death. I, once so full of life, became timid and retiring, sensitive to an excessive degree. One look was enough to reduce me to tears, and the only way I was content was to be left alone completely.[6]

Things did not improve for Thérèse when she started school at the Benedictine Abbey near her home. Again, in her own words we glimpse the agony of those years: 'I have often heard it said that the time spent at school is the best and happiest of one's life. It wasn't this way for me. The five years I spent in school were the saddest in my life'.[7]

Unlike Francis, who did not excel in academic studies at school, Thérèse was more advanced in learning than the other children of her age. She was nearly always first in her class and on one occasion

Thérèse relates that the priest, Father Domin, called her 'his little doctor' because of the way in which Thérèse grasped and understood what was being taught.[8]

In adolescence both Francis and Thérèse dreamed of achieving great feats of valour and heroism. After the example of the warrior saint George, Francis turned his thoughts and deeds to chivalry and knighthood in search of personal glory and honour in this world, while Thérèse chose the warrior saint Joan of Arc as a model and example. Thérèse, unlike Francis, turned her thoughts and deeds to Carmel where personal heroism was mostly hidden and glory was neither sought nor given at a personal level. This required a different kind of heroism. Yet both had a passion for the possible and a determination to make dreams a reality.

Francis and Thérèse: Journeys and Dreams

When Francis was nineteen years old and at the height of his youthful fame and popularity within his peer group, civil war broke out between Assisi and Perugia and lasted from 1201–1209. Fired with youthful enthusiasm and seeking military glory, Francis enlisted for battle and in 1202 the opposing armies met on the banks of the Collestrada. Perugia conquered Assisi and Francis was taken prisoner and remained in prison for a year. This journey into war shattered Francis's dreams—at least for a while. His experience in prison affected his delicate health and his father paid a ransom for his release. A long convalescence followed.

Shattered dreams usually cause upheaval, disappointment, disorientation and at times depression. If worked through, such experiences can lead to the discovery of new insights, new meanings, new challenges, new depths in prayer and greater determination. So it was for Francis. His biographer tells us that he prayed very earnestly to God to show him the way he should go and to teach him to do his will. A terrible struggle was going on in his soul causing him great anguish and suffering.[9]

Eventually Francis regained his equilibrium and once again dreams of worldly fame and honour assailed him. In 1205, at the age of twenty-three, Francis was fired with enthusiasm and joined the ranks of Count Gentile's army, hoping to win renown and public acclaim. It was not to be. The Lord intervened. Francis was challenged and the challenge came in the course of two separate dreams, which had a momentous influence on the young Francis and far reaching consequences for his future. We shall return to this point later. Renouncing worldly fame and honour, Francis surrendered to the Lord and redirected all his energies to God's glory and honour.

Did the young Thérèse have dreams of personal glory and honour? She herself relates that God in his mercy intervened in her life, otherwise she might have become a very proud and worldly young woman, seduced by the pleasures and vainglory the world has to offer. Again, in her own words, Thérèse writes of a holiday trip when she revisited Alençon after some years in Lisieux:

> I can say that it was during my stay at Alençon that I made my first entrance into the world. Everything was joy and happiness around me; I was entertained, coddled, and admired; in a word, my life during those two weeks was

> strewn only with flowers. I must admit this type
> of life had its charms for me.[10]

Even at the tender age of ten years, Thérèse saw through worldly vanity and ambition and she attributed her pursuit of truth and the glory of God to the working of grace.

Thérèse had dreams of glory but they were not in the realm of self-glory or vainglory in this world. They were dreams of sainthood involving a way of life that would give all the glory to God. These dreams began at a very early age and were to shape her life, message and mission with a fascination and magnetism that continues to enthral. Thérèse is bold in stating 'I considered that I was born for glory' and then goes on to explain that her "glory" was in becoming a great Saint, hidden during her lifetime but recognised after her death. As the saying goes: the rest is history!

Francis and Thérèse: The Call

The experience of receiving a call from God is very personal. For some people, like St Francis, it may be a series of dramatic, unusual and significant events that unexpectedly break into everyday life and experience. For others, like Thérèse it may be a gentle, strong, pervasive whisper that mounts in intensity as time passes. The journey may include significant and insightful moments of a more 'ordinary' and domestic nature, but they are nevertheless decisive growth moments within the call. What they have in common is the inner conviction that leads to the same goal: total surrender, total union and total transformation in a love that knows no bounds.

God's personal call to Francis came in several decisive encounters: two dreams with invitations and challenges, hearing the voice of Christ from the San Damiano Crucifix and a meeting with a leper. All of these had dramatic effects on the young Francis and each of them shaped his life, his vocation, his message, his mission and his prevailing relevance for the Church and the world throughout the centuries. Let us look very briefly at each of these moments in the life of Francis and discover the essence of the call and the response that led Francis to the heights of sanctity.

Francis and Dreams of Glory

Inspired by the ambition to become a knight and attain fame and glory in the service of the Pope and the Church, Francis set out for war. In the course of his journey Francis had a dream. In his dream he saw a palace filled with all the trappings of war: shields, spears and all the weapons that had significance in a military conquest. In his dream Francis heard a voice telling him that all these weapons were for him and his knights. This dream filled Francis with renewed enthusiasm and zeal for a military career, bringing him the desired honour and glory in the public arena. On awakening Francis exclaimed: 'I know I will become a great prince'.[11]

The second dream of Francis challenged him to reassess his interpretation of the first dream in terms of God's dream for Francis. In his second dream Francis heard a voice asking him where he was going and what his plans and ambitions were. A conversation then took place between Francis and his Lord, the outcome of which was to change his life forever. The voice said: 'Who can do more good for you? The lord or the servant?' When Francis answered him: "The lord", he again said to him: "Then why are you abandoning the lord for the servant, the patron for the client?" And Francis said: "Lord, what do you want me to do?" "Go back to your land," he said, "and what you are to do will be told to you. You must understand in another way the vision which you saw"'.[12] Everything was not revealed at once for Francis. He, like us, had to wait on the Lord's gradual revelation of his plan for his life. What he did know was that dreams of worldly fame and glory were no longer part of that plan. So Francis gave up his military ambitions and returned to Assisi.

Francis and Leper Encounters

Accustomed as he was to a life of luxury and peer companions of choice, Francis now faced a reversal of values that turned his life upside down. That he found lepers nauseating and repulsive to his sensitivity is well known. Before his conversion, he would go out of his way to avoid seeing or meeting them. He himself states: 'When I was in sin, it seemed to me extremely bitter to see lepers'. Then the moment of decision came. Francis met a leper. Recognising that the Lord had led him to this encounter, touched by grace and eager to change, Francis embraced the leper as a brother and from that moment on 'What had previously seemed bitter was changed into sweetness'.[13] But there was still a long road ahead. God's dream for Francis was unfolding in gradual, albeit dramatic encounters.

Francis and A Talking Crucifix

While Francis was still searching for the Lord's will he visited a small broken-down Church of San Damiano to pray. Amid the confusion and darkness in the depths of his heart there was a very genuine desire to know and do God's will. This was Francis prayer before the San Damiano Crucifix:

> Most high, glorious God, enlighten the darkness of my heart, and give me true faith, certain hope, and perfect charity, sense and knowledge, that I may carry out Your holy and true command.[14]

The crucified and risen Christ on the Cross, answered the prayer of Francis by asking him to 'Go and rebuild My Church'. Being entrusted with so great a privilege and responsibility, Francis was overjoyed and, moved to his innermost depths, he decided to start the repair work immediately. This was another step on the journey for Francis, the wider implications not yet within his grasp.

Reflecting on the initial call of Francis we have seen that the unconscious (his dreams), his reaching out to those on the margins of society (the lepers), and his personal relationship of call and response in prayerful dialogue with Christ (the San Damiano Crucifix), were key factors in shaping the personal vocation that would emerge with a message and mission of perennial value.

Thérèse and Dreams of Glory

Like Francis, Thérèse too had dreams of glory but unlike Francis she did not begin with a desire for worldly fame and honour. From a very early age Thérèse set her sights on heavenly glory and boldly saw her name written in the heavens. Let us listen to her own words as a child:

> I would gaze upon the stars which were twinkling ever so peacefully in the skies and the sight carried me away. There was especially one cluster of *golden pearls* which attracted my attention and gave me great joy because they were in the form of a 'T'. I pointed them out to Papa and told him my name was written in heaven.[15]

Later when she entered Carmel, Thérèse understood that human eyes would not see her glory during her life on earth. Nevertheless she was undaunted in her conviction and bold confidence that she would become not just a Saint, but also a great Saint! We will speak more of this dream of glory later as her message and mission unfolds.

Thérèse and her Magic Shoes

Like Francis, Thérèse had her special moment that marked a transition point in her call and her faith journey. It happened at Christmas when she was nearly fourteen and Thérèse refers to it as her Christmas grace. It was a family custom for young French children to have their shoes filled with presents which would be opened after midnight Mass. Thérèse refers to her 'magic shoes' and recalls how this particular year she overheard her father say he would be glad when she outgrew this childish custom. The over sensitive Thérèse would normally have cried profusely and suffered intensely over such a remark. That Christmas was different. Thérèse says she grew up because she responded to a special grace, which she refers to as 'my complete conversion'. She remarks: 'The work I was unable to do in ten years was done by Jesus in one instant, contenting himself with my *good will* which was never lacking'.[16] This Christmas grace led Thérèse to a more intense desire to forget herself and become 'a fisher of souls' and her opportunity came in a most unexpected way.

Thérèse and the Thirst of Jesus

Similar to Francis before the San Damiano Cross, Thérèse too was moved by Christ on the Cross. She recalls a significant encounter in these words:

> One Sunday, looking at a picture of our Lord on the Cross, I was struck by the blood flowing from one of the divine hands. I felt a pang of great sorrow thinking this blood was falling to the ground without anyone's hastening to gather it up. I was resolved to remain in spirit at the foot of the cross and to receive the divine dew. I understood that I was then to pour it out on souls. The cry of Jesus on the cross sounded continually in my heart: '*I thirst!*'.[17]

At this stage of Thérèse discerning her call, she felt an intense desire to reach out to sinners, the criminals, and the condemned. Then a special moment of grace and decision came for Thérèse. There was a condemned criminal named Pranzini, who was going to die impenitent and Thérèse could not bear the thought of such a destiny so she prayed for mercy for him and asked for a sign that her prayer had been granted. Contrary to all expectations, at the last moment Pranzini grasped a crucifix and kissed Christ's wounds three times. From that moment, Thérèse was confirmed in her call to pray for mercy for all poor sinners.

Francis and Thérèse: The Message

When we look at the initial call of Francis and Thérèse, what if anything have they in common? We have highlighted three aspects that seem to be significant factors in their early development: dreams of glory, love of the marginalized of society—those who are poor in the eyes of the world, and a sensitive heart to the suffering Christ and his thirst for rebuilding lives that are broken by creating loving relationships. These three aspects of their call will weave like a golden thread through their journeys of development and each will express them with a genius and originality that still inspires and refreshes.

Both Francis and Thérèse laboured wholeheartedly for the glory of God: Francis on the road as an itinerant preacher of the Gospel and brother to lepers, creating brotherhood and sisterhood as the special mark of his charismatic gift to the Church and the world. This language of fraternity, rooted in the Fatherhood of God, in a family where we are all brothers and sisters with our brother, Christ, is the hallmark of Francis's gift, genius and originality. The way he related to every person as brother and sister, in his or her uniqueness, the way he related to the whole of creation as brother and sister makes Francis a little brother to all, irrespective of age, creed, culture or religion: a man with a universal appeal who desires to be a brother to all.

In contrast to Francis the itinerant preacher, Thérèse lived her short life in an enclosed Carmelite Convent, unknown to the world at large, hidden, loving, generous, prayerful and self-sacrificing to a heroic degree, yet embracing the whole world as her cloister. Hers was a thirst to make the love and mercy of Jesus known to every person in such a way that each was capable of responding and receiving according to each one's God-given capacity. Thérèse believed that God Himself taught her a Gospel wisdom that is rooted in being a child of the Father—as every person is a child of the same Father, the Creator of all. If each is a child of the Father then we are all sisters and brothers in Christ. In a way that is different from Francis, Thérèse becomes a little sister to all, irrespective of age, creed, culture or religion: a woman with a universal appeal who desires to draw all into the family of God.

The message of Francis and Thérèse is the Gospel message of God's extravagant love and mercy, especially to the 'little ones' of this world. This is exemplified in the way in which both Saints lived their lives and presented their message: Francis as a little brother, a brother minor; Thérèse and her Little Way. Love and littleness are the hallmarks of their Gospel message. How this love and littleness are expressed and become a special charism within the Church will be explored throughout this book.

Francis and Thérèse: The Mission

Initially Francis seemed to be unaware of a call that involved a wider mission within the Church and the world. He desired to love the God of Love and responded by rebuilding broken down churches so that places of worship were restored for the glory of God. This first step was part and parcel of the hermit's call and Francis worked enthusiastically to labour in this way for the Lord. It was only much later that Francis realised that 'The Lord gave me brothers' and this would shape his personal call and vocation in such a way that the poor little man of Assisi brought to birth a new family within the Church that was, and is, all-embracing in its fraternal love restoring broken relationships with the whole of humanity and with the whole of creation. His being a brother had a particular and unique expression: a brother minor, that is, a little or lesser brother. And Francis believed this call to be brother minor was directly from God, saying that the Lord willed and revealed to him that they were to be called Lesser Brothers.[18]

Thérèse on the other hand had a burning desire to love the God of Love and to make him loved on all five Continents. She seemed to have an intuitive grasp of a God given call to reach all peoples to the end of the earth and the end of time. She was also given two priests to be her special 'brothers' in the work of saving souls and bringing them to God. These were missionary Priests for whom Thérèse would pray and make sacrifices in an act of faith and solidarity with the Body of Christ. She could do this by her Little Way of love of which we will say more later. Thérèse firmly believed that the love and zeal of a Carmelite should embrace the whole world and she herself describes her personal vocation in these glowing terms:

> O Jesus, my Love ... my *vocation*, at last I have found it ... my vocation is love! Yes, I have found my place in the Church and it is You, O my God, who have given me this place; in the heart of the Church, my Mother, I shall be *Love*. Thus I shall be everything, and thus my dream will be realized'.[19]

Not only did Thérèse believe she had a mission to give this Gospel message to the Church and the world, she believed in her God-given mission to make it known to a legion of souls in such a way that she would spend her heaven doing good upon earth—and this until the end of time.

How fortunate we are to have the written words and prayers of both these Saints. How fortunate we are to have dictated writings that reflect their thoughts and attitudes. How fortunate we are to have so many 'lives' of both Francis and Thérèse that give us new insights and inspiration. How fortunate we are to have two well-established spiritual families within the Church—the Franciscans and the Carmelites—who continue to share the Gospel way of life upon which both spiritualities are founded. Their lives live on, their message pulses with newness and fullness of life, their relevance is timeless.

Francis and Thérèse: Their Relevance

The Franciscan way of Minority and the Theresian Little Way have been handed down to us through the lives and personal examples of Francis and Thérèse. As a Friar Minor, Francis became brother to all without exception. As a Carmelite, Thérèse became a sister to all through her Little Way from which no one—not even the smallest, weakest soul is exempt. All-embracing in their invitation to follow the Gospel path of love and littleness, Francis and Thérèse are among those souls of whom Pope John Paul II speaks when he visited Lisieux in 1980: 'Saints never grow old. They never become figures of the past, men and women of 'yesterday'. On the contrary, they are always men and women of the future, witnesses of the world to come'.

The question now is: How are Francis and Thérèse relevant for twenty-first century people and how do we tap into their spirituality in a way that is accessible to all? We have already mentioned that we have their own writings and this perhaps is a first step in getting to know them. We can then access the Franciscan and Carmelite traditions through the writings of those who lived with the Saints and wrote about them. Again the documents available are numerous.

This little book is only an introduction to these two great Saints who make the Gospel message a universal call to love in a way that is personal, practical and applicable to all. I believe Francis and Thérèse are outstanding role models for people in every walk of life. I believe they have much in common because their focus is love and littleness, which is a perennial Gospel message, rooted in the Person of Jesus Christ to whom Francis and Thérèse were devoted. But the way in which they lived their own personal vocation expresses the wonder and dignity, the originality and uniqueness of every person in his or her relationship with God.

St Francis has a message that the world of today is hungering to hear and, in the eight hundred anniversary of the approval of the Franciscan way of life within the Church, much has been done and continues to be done to unearth the treasures of the Franciscan tradition. One eminent scholar, Zachary Hayes believes that the Franciscan tradition is a treasure that has much to offer for the healing of humanity and the world at large. How pertinent that we tap into such a treasure at this moment in history especially as it relates to the Person of Jesus Christ, the dignity of the human person and the care of creation.

The Little Way of St Thérèse has also been described as a way of life with universal appeal and relevance. These are the words of Pope John Paul II when he proclaimed St Thérèse a Doctor of the Church: 'Thérèse possesses an exceptional universality. Her person, the Gospel message of the "Little Way" of trust and spiritual childhood have received and continue to receive a remarkable welcome, which has transcended every border.'[20]

Pope John Paul goes on to say that the influence of her message extends to the Church's pastors, to experts in theology and spirituality, to priests and seminarians, to men and women religious, to ecclesial movements and new communities, to men and women of every condition and every continent. To everyone Thérèse gives her personal confirmation that the Christian mystery, whose witness and apostle she became by making herself in prayer 'the apostle of the apostles', as she boldly calls herself must be taken literally, with the greatest possible realism, because it has a value for every time and place. The power of her message lies in its concrete explanation of how all Jesus's promises are fulfilled in the believer who knows how confidently to welcome in his or her own life the saving presence of the Redeemer.

Having briefly introduced our two Saints of universal appeal, we will root Francis and Thérèse in a Gospel spirituality that marked their lives and universal message. Their love of Scripture was the foundation of all they said and did. This love of the word of God led them to embrace and emulate the Word made flesh in Jesus Christ and they did this in their own unique and God-given way; yet we find striking similarities in their expression and lived experience of the Word of God. Though separated by gender, time, country and culture, Francis and Thérèse reveal 'that charism of Gospel wisdom' of which Pope John Paul II speaks:

> Mother Church also rejoices in noting that throughout history the Lord has continued to reveal himself to the little and the humble, enabling his chosen ones, through the Spirit

who 'searches everything, even the depths of God' (1 Co 2:10).[21]

This will form the basis of our reflections in the next chapter.

Reflection

Considering your own name, background, cultural influences, points of conversion and transition, and early dreams for your life, who has influenced you on your journey of faith?

Notes

[1]   J. Clarke, OCD, (Trans.) *Story of a Soul: The Autobiography of St Thérèse of Lisieux,* (Washington D.C.: ICS Publication, 1976), p. 5.

[2]   G. Gaucher, *The Spiritual Journey of Thérèse of Lisieux,* (London: Darton Longman Todd, 1987), p. 13.

[3]   P. Descouvemont, (Text) H. N. Loose, (Photographs) *Thérèse and Lisieux,* (Canada: Novalis MI: Eerdmans, Dublin: Veritas, 1996), p. 10.

[4]   H. U. von Balthasar, *Two Sisters in the Spirit,* (San Francisco: Ignatius Press, 1992), p. 21.

[5]   R. J. Armstrong, OFMCap, W. J. A. Hellmann OFM Conv, W. J. Short, OFM *Francis Of Assisi The Founder Early Documents,* vol. I, (London, New York: New City Press, 2000), p.194.

[6]   Clarke, *Story of a Soul,* p. 35.

[7]   *Ibid.,* p. 53.

[8]   *Ibid.,* p. 81.

[9]   Armstrong *et al., The Saint,* vol. I, p. 187.

[10] Clarke,. OCD., *Story of a Soul,* p. 73.

[11] R. J. Armstrong, OFM Cap, Hellmann, W. J. A. OFM Conv, Short, W. J. OFM, *Francis Of Assisi The Founder Early Documents,* vol. II, (London, New York: New City Press, 2000), p. 71.

[12] *Ibid.,* p. 71.

13 *Ibid.*
14 Armstrong et al., *Francis of Assisi*, vol. I, p. 40.
15 Clarke, *Story of a Soul*, p. 43.
16 *Ibid.*, p. 98.
17 *Ibid.*, p. 99.
18 R. J. Armstrong, OFM Cap, Hellmann, W. J. A. OFM Conv, Short, W. J. OFM, *Francis Of Assisi The Prophet Early Documents*, vol. III, (London, New York: New City Press, 2001), p. 276.
19 Clarke, *Story of a Soul*, p. 194.
20 Pope John Paul II, *Divini Amoris Scientia*, 1.
21 *Ibid.*

Chapter 2

Living in the World of Gospel Gift

No one showed me what I should do, but the Most High Himself revealed to me that I should live according to the pattern of the Holy Gospel.[1]

St Francis

To keep Jesus's word — that is the sole condition of our happiness, the proof of our love for him. But what is this word? It seems to me that Jesus's word is Himself. Jesus, the Word, the Word of God![2]

St Thérèse

T he lives and spirituality of Francis and Thérèse are rooted in sacred Scripture, and in the Word made flesh, Jesus Christ. Neither wrote learned treatises on Gospel spirituality or how to live the Christian life; rather they incarnate in their lives the message they proclaim. Francis and Thérèse were radically committed to 'doing' the Gospel in the ordinariness of day-to-day living. This they did with an originality and genius that reveals the uniqueness of the Gospel message in every human life. Yet the medium and the message are not identical.

> Even when the man or woman and the message complement each other, they never coincide totally. Each of us possesses his/her own personality, significance, destiny and role... personal experience simply serves as a starting-point and basis for a spiritual doctrine that is valid for everyone.[3]

In essence, it is a radical stance and a radical challenge to find one's true self and identity. Francis and Thérèse realised that such a discovery is founded on a relationship with, and understanding of, the God-man Jesus Christ, a relationship that is nurtured by the word of God. Therefore, they immersed themselves in the word of God and became for all time a little 'word' within the Word, inviting others to do the same within their own individual call and gift. In this way, Francis and Thérèse had no desire to draw attention to themselves. Their focus was Jesus, the revelation of the Father in whose heart each of us finds our inner truth and identity. Yet their approach to the word can teach and inspire every person to embrace the word of God in an encounter that has potential to change one's life forever.

The Word of God and the Call of Francis

Francis had a profound love and reverence for the word of God and this is very evident from his own writings and the writings of his biographers. At the very beginning of his search for the will of God, Francis heard the word of God proclaimed at Mass in the little church of the Portiuncula and from that moment he could say: 'This is what I want; this is what I seek; this is what I desire with all my heart'.[4] The passage that evoked this heartfelt, enthusiastic and generous response was from the Gospel of Matthew. 'Provide yourselves with no gold or silver, not even with coppers for your purses, with no haversack for the journey or spare tunic or footwear or a staff, for the labourer deserves his keep' (10:9–10). His biographer, friar Celano, goes on to say that Francis was no deaf hearer of the Gospel. What he had heard he immediately put into practice.

When others wished to join Francis in his Gospel way of life, he sought further direction in the word of God. We have the example of his visit to the church of Saint Nicholas in Assisi. He went there with his first companions, Bernard of Quintavalle and Peter 'to seek counsel from the Lord' regarding their way of life. It is interesting that Francis and Bernard had been discussing the Gospel passage on renunciation but because they were simple, they did not know how to find the passage in the Gospel about renunciation. Intuitively Francis knew his Gospel call but with his companions he sought further revelation and confirmation in the word of God.

Entering the church, they prayed devoutly that the Lord would show them his will, and in honour of the Blessed Trinity Francis decided to open the book of the

Gospels randomly three times, to seek there their form of life. At the first opening of the book their eyes fell upon a text from the Gospel of Matthew: 'If you want to be perfect, go, sell all that you have, and give to the poor' (19:21). On opening the book a second time their eyes fell upon the text from the Gospel of Luke: 'Take nothing on your journey' (9:3) and on the third opening they read from Matthew: 'If anyone wishes to come after me, let him deny himself and take up his cross and follow me' (16:24). This threefold testimony confirmed for Francis the Gospel foundation for a life of poverty. Overjoyed by the texts he randomly found, he said to his companions: 'This is our life and rule'.[5] Another text that relates the same incident has Francis exclaim with great joy: 'This is what we want. This is what we were seeking. This will be our rule'.[6] Francis was confident that the Lord would reveal and confirm in his word what he already sensed in his heart. And so it was.

Towards the end of his life, when Francis wrote his Testament, with personal conviction he confidently proclaimed: 'No one showed me what I should do, but the Most High Himself revealed to me that I should live according to the pattern of the Holy Gospel'.[7] Later we will explore the lived reality and particular emphasis the Gospel would take in shaping the life of Francis and his followers.

Throughout his life, Francis turned to the word of God for direction, consolation and counsel. Towards the end of his life when he was in solitude for forty days on Mount La Verna preparing for the feast of St Michael, his biographer, St Bonaventure states: 'Through a divine sign from heaven he had learned that, in opening the book of the Gospel, Christ would reveal to him what God considered most acceptable in him and from him'.[8] Bonaventure then goes on to say that Francis prayed with great devotion, before placing the sacred book on the altar, to enter more deeply in the will of God. As on a previous occasion in the church of St Nicholas, Francis opened the sacred book three times in the name of the Holy Trinity. Significantly, three times the page opened at a text from the passion of Jesus. From this, Francis intuited that just as he had entered into and imitated the actions in the life of the incarnate Christ, now God was asking that he should enter into the suffering and passion of Christ.

Within the forty day solitude experience of Francis on Mount La Verna, Francis was totally transformed into the likeness of Christ crucified, sharing in his passion and receiving his precious wounds in his weak and frail body. 'O truly the most Christian of men, who strove by perfect imitation to be conformed while living to Christ living, dying to Christ dying, and dead to Christ dead, and deserved to be adorned with an expressed likeness!'.[9]

The Word of God and the Call of Thérèse

Thérèse, like Francis, discovered her identity and personal vocation in the word of God. It is obvious from her writings that Thérèse was very familiar with many texts from Scripture. She seems to have developed a sense of the living power of the word in such a way that she could paraphrase and express herself from within the word. At the tender age when she experienced the call to Carmel and was due to visit, she couched it in the language of the Song of Songs. 'The morning of the day I was to visit I was thinking things over in my bed for it was there I made my profound meditations, and, contrary to the bride in the Canticles, I always found my Beloved there.'[10] This is markedly obvious in her Autobiography where there are many references that are partially quoted or paraphrased to express her call and identification from within the word of God.

By frequently consulting the word of God, Thérèse grew in her understanding of herself and her God-given vocation. Scripture was the foundation for her identity, her prayer, her message and her mission. We are fortunate in having Thérèse's own words regarding the significance of the word of God in her life. At the age of fourteen she experienced the thirst of Jesus on the cross and she took steps to alleviate that thirst in a very practical way. 'The cry of Jesus on the Cross sounded continually in my heart: "I thirst". These words ignited within me an unknown and very living fire….as yet, it was not the souls of priests that attracted me, but those of great sinners'.[11] We have already referred to that story in chapter one in the context of Thérèse reaching out to those on the edges of society. Now in the context of her call, we can see how the word of God shaped Thérèse to take practical steps in response to the word and to alleviate the thirst of Jesus.

Years of searching, savouring, pondering and praying the word of God, would eventually lead Thérèse, to discover her own 'Little Way'. Thérèse first lived the word she pondered and prayed, then at the age of nineteen, she eventually developed and articulated the word of God in a way that not only gave her a clearer self-identity and mission, but would also resonate with universal significance to other 'little souls'. The essence was contained in the call to little-ness with the confidence of a very little child. 'Whoever is a little one, let him come to me' (Pr 9:4), and 'As a mother caresses her child, so I will comfort you. I will carry you on my bosom and I will dandle you on my knees' (Is 66:12–13).

It was later in her life that Thérèse would experience that momentous thrill of recognition of her God-given uniqueness within the Body of Christ. And it came when she was reading and searching the Word of God. This is how Thérèse shares her experience of that precious and unforgettable moment.

> During my meditation, my desires caused me a veritable martyrdom, and I opened the Epis-tles of St Paul to find some kind of answer. Chapters 12 and 13 of the First Epistle to Corin-thians fell under my eyes. I read there, in the first of these chapters, that *all* cannot be apos-tles, prophets, doctors, etc., that the Church is composed of different members, and that the eye cannot be the hand *at one and the same time* ... Without becoming discouraged, I continued my reading, and this sentence consoled me: *"Yet strive after THE BETTER GIFTS, and I point out to you a yet more excellent way"*. And the Apostle explains how all *the most PERFECT gifts* are nothing without *LOVE*. That charity is the excellent way that leads most surely to God.
>
> *I finally had rest. Considering the mystical body of the Church, I had not recognised myself in any of the members described by St Paul, or rather I desired to find myself in them all ...I understood that the Church had a heart and that this heart was burning with love. In the excess of my delirious joy, I cried*

out: O Jesus, my love ... my vocation, at last I have found it ... MY VOCATION IS LOVE.[12]

Recognising the biblical foundation of their call, let us now explore the different ways in which Francis and Thérèse approached the word of God in their deepening relationship with God.

Francis: Approach to the Word of God

The word of God was central and transformative in the life and prayer of Francis. For this to become a reality in our lives too, it is helpful to appreciate the way in which Francis approached the word of God. Let us begin with his own words where Francis distinguishes between the letter that kills and the spirit that gives life.

> The apostle says: The letter kills, but the spirit gives life. Those people are put to death by the letter who only wish to know the words alone, that they might be esteemed wiser than others and be able to acquire great riches to give to their relatives and friends. And those religious are put to death by the letter who are not willing to follow the spirit of the divine letter but, instead, wish only to know the words and to interpret them for others.
>
> And those people are brought to life by the spirit of the divine letter who do not attribute every letter they know, or wish to know, to the body but, by words and example, return them to the Most High to Whom every good belongs.[13]

In this *Admonition*, Francis is making a clear distinction between the person who wishes to know the word of God for personal gain, popularity or status and the person who desires to know the word of God in order to put it into practice in his or her own life and return glory to God in doing so. This *Admonition* was of the utmost importance to Francis because his form of life, revealed to him from the Most High, was based on the Gospel. The life giving words of sacred scripture called him to follow in the footsteps of Jesus the Word made flesh. If the written words do not lead to this identification with Jesus, then they are indeed dead words. That Francis wished to delve deeper into the meaning of the precious words of scripture is obvious and he held in high esteem those who helped others to do so. Towards the end of his life, Francis said to the brothers: 'And we must honour all theologians and those who minister the most holy divine words and respect them as those who minister spirit and life'.[14]

Spirit and life! Francis realised with heartfelt conviction that the words of scripture were Spirit-filled and life giving. Entering the depth of meaning contained in the word leads to ever deepening love and identification with the Word made flesh, Jesus Christ. Humility, poverty, littleness and love were the hallmarks of the fraternal life of Francis and his followers as they savoured every precious word on the pages of scripture. In fact Francis made sure that each brother had just that: a page to savour from sacred scripture. St Bonaventure, one of his later biographers, tells the charming story of Francis sharing the word of God — literally!

> That you might appreciate how much the study of Holy Scripture delighted St Francis, let me tell you what I myself heard from a brother who is still living. Once a New Testament came into Francis's hands, and since so many brothers could

not use it all at once, he pulled the leaves apart and distributed the pages among them. Thus each could read it and not be a hindrance to others.[15]

Francis: Taught from Within

St Bonaventure captures the essence of Francis as a Gospel person and confirms for us his great love and reverence for the word of God. He tells us that Francis was not educated in scholarly disciplines indicating that he was not an academic with theological qualifications. Rather, Francis was taught from within, by the Spirit of God with a wisdom that was a special grace and gift from God. As a result, Francis had a very deep understanding of the meaning and significance of the word of God. This knowledge from within is what we might call knowledge of the heart. Bonaventure tells us that whatever Francis put into his mind through his reading of the word of God, he wrote indelibly in his heart. 'His genius, pure and unstained, penetrated hidden mysteries. Where the knowledge of teachers is outside, the passion of the lover entered'.[16]

Francis heard the word of God with great reverence and attentiveness. He then lovingly digested and savoured it in his heart. We are told that he mulled over the words with great reverence and devotion after which he would put them into practice. In other words Francis 'was no deaf hearer of the Gospel; rather he committed everything he heard to his excellent memory and was careful to carry it out to the letter'.[17] In this way nothing was wasted because he allowed the word of God to take hold of him and transform his life. This is why it is sometimes remarked that Francis 'did' the Gospel. In his personal and positive response to the Gospel, Francis is a living witness to what Pope

Benedict refers to in his Encyclical *Spe Salvi*. The Pope asks the question: 'Can our encounter with the God who in Christ, has shown us His face and opened his heart, be for us too not just "informative" but "performative" — that is to say, can it change our lives?'[18] The Gospel did change the life of Francis. His 'was the fruitful way to read and learn, rather than wander through a thousand treatises'.[19]

St Bonaventure was a very learned friar within the family of Francis and he was very impressed when a learned Doctor of sacred theology discussed with Francis certain aspects of scripture, which were very difficult to understand. Bonaventure, referring to Francis's God-given wisdom in penetrating the truth of the word of God and his constant endeavour to put it into practice, said: 'He often untangled the ambiguities of questions and brought the hidden to light'.[20] This depth of understanding Bonaventure ascribed to Francis's imitation of Christ. In other words, he put the words into practice by carrying out in his activity the perfect truth described in them.

This is a wonderful description of Francis's living of the Gospel and his understanding of, and approach to, the word of God. We have emphasis on the gift of inner wisdom given from God. We have emphasis on love as the motivation and central factor in his encounter with the word. We have attentiveness and savouring of the word. We have emphasis on the place of the heart in his memorizing of the word. Finally we have the power of the word to transform when it becomes fruitful in action, imitation and application. In other words, the word of God was, for Francis, an entry into and penetration of the divine mysteries leading him into closer union with Jesus his beloved Lord. The brothers noticed this passionate love for Jesus in the heart of Francis.

> He was always with Jesus:
> Jesus in his heart,
> Jesus in his mouth,
> Jesus in his ears,
> Jesus in his eyes,
> Jesus in his hands,
> he bore Jesus always in his whole body.[21]

Francis: The Word is a Seed

From what has already been said, we could get the impression that for Francis, listening to the word of God, savouring it in his heart and putting it into practice in his life was relatively easy. Not so. Francis knew from experience how difficult it is to allow God to bring forth fruit in patience. We have only to read Chapter 22 in the First Rule of St Francis to catch a glimpse of the struggle within his heart to persevere in his on-going encounter with the word of God and the challenges involved.[22]

In this Chapter 22 of the Rule, Francis presents us with a unique composition of the parable of the Sower based on the Synoptic Gospels: Mt 13, Mk 4 and Lk 8. With genius and originality, Francis pieces together various phrases from the parable of the Sower from the three Gospels and then presents them with the theological insights on discipleship as found in St John's Gospel. It is truly an amazing teaching from the word of God that reveals Francis's profound insight and wisdom into the living word of God. It is worth developing this point in a little more depth to show in a practical way the realities and challenges involved because Francis speaks of Satan's subtlety, malice and ensnarement when a person tries to live by and in the word of God.

In his approach to the word of God, Francis speaks of the necessity of care and attention because Satan tries to distract us from the word in ways that are subtle and malicious. He also expands on this by stating quite clearly that Satan wishes 'to choke out the word and precepts of the Lord from our memory'.[23] This is interesting in the light of what we have already said about Francis learning by heart many passages of scripture. St Bonaventure remarks that whenever Francis read the word of God 'he imprinted it tenaciously on his memory'.[24] Therefore the words of Jesus in the parable of the Sower are very important for Francis, especially in relation to the word as a seed that needs nurturing with the greatest care and attention so that it takes root in the heart.

Keen awareness that the word of God has to find a home in the human heart, in the very depths of the human person, urged Francis to share his understanding of the parable with his brothers. His teaching in this Chapter from the Rule is very insightful especially in his recognition of the type of soil into which the seed, that is, the word of God falls. At the very outset Francis tells us to be very careful about the kind of soil we cultivate in our hearts. There is discipline involved here. For Francis this is all- important because the seed is the word of God and we have a personal responsibility for its reception, growth and eventual fruitfulness in a life of radical discipleship, the latter outlined particularly in St John's Gospel with emphasis on the indwelling of the Trinity. Two references are of interest in our present context: 'If you make my word your home you will indeed be my disciples; you will come to know the truth, and the truth will set you free' (Jn 8:32) and 'Anyone who loves me will keep my word, and my Father will love him and we shall come to him and make a home in him' (Jn 14:23).

A careful reading of the biblical texts quoted above from the Synoptic Gospels (Mt 13, Mk 4 and Lk 8) alongside Francis's own interpretation and exposition in Chapter 22 of his Rule, reveals a strategy for receiving the word: hearing, understanding, holding onto, bringing forth fruit and persevering.[25] That Francis put this into practice in his own life is clearly evident especially when, towards the end of his life, Francis was in great pain and a brother reminded him that he had always taken refuge in the scriptures. The brother offered to read him some text but Francis replied:

> It is good to read the testimonies of scripture, and it is good to seek the Lord our God in them. But I have already taken in more than enough for meditating and reflecting. I do not need more, my son; I know Christ, poor and crucified.[26]

We cannot underestimate the importance of familiarity with the word of God that led Francis to such personal identification with the Word, Jesus Christ.

Francis knew the Scriptures so well, especially the Gospels and the Psalms, that he composed his own *Office of the Passion*, combining different texts into a very personal, prayerful reflection on his crucified Lord. He seems to have had a great freedom and flexibility in weaving different texts for his own prayerful purposes. His faithfulness to the Divine Office is well documented and it is this faithfulness that nurtured such loving familiarity with the Psalms. 'And although I may be simple and infirm, I nevertheless want to have a cleric always with me who will celebrate the Office with me as it is prescribed in the Rule'.[27]

Francis's love of the word of God led him to total union with Jesus, especially in the love and littleness manifested though poverty and suffering. We are told that it was Francis's highest aim, foremost desire, and greatest intention to pay heed to the holy Gospel in all things and through all things, to follow the teaching of our Lord Jesus Christ. This he did on a daily basis, paying particular and careful attention to the Psalter and to the readings of the day that are proclaimed at Mass. Even when it was not possible for him to attend Mass he asked a brother to read the Gospel of the day.

In death, Francis requested that the Gospel of St John be read to him beginning with the account of the Last Supper. Significantly, the brother had already opened the book and his eyes fell upon the exact passage that Francis had requested. In this brief account of Francis and his love of the word of God, the words of the Franciscan scholar, Dominic Monti seem very apt:

> Francis has heard the Scriptures in such a way that their many words have been condensed into the Person of Christ, and not all the many possible interpretations of the person of Jesus, but into two episodes—his humble birth and his painful death'.[28]

We will develop these themes in later chapters. The purpose here is to emphasise the Gospel foundation of Francis's life, message, mission and relevance. Let us now turn to Thérèse and her approach to the word of God.

Thérèse: Taught from Within

Like Francis, the word of God is central in understanding Thérèse's life, message, mission and relevance. This was highlighted when she was proclaimed a Doctor of the Church in 1997. Pope John Paul II spoke of Thérèse and her special charism of Gospel wisdom in the following words:

> During her life Thérèse discovered 'new lights, hidden and mysterious meanings' and received from the divine Teacher that 'science of love'

> which she then expressed with particular origi-
> nality in her writings. This science is the
> luminous expression of her knowledge of the
> mystery of the kingdom and of her personal
> experience of grace. It can be considered a special
> charism of Gospel wisdom which Thérèse, like
> other saints and teachers of faith, attained in
> prayer.[29]

Neither Francis nor Thérèse had any particular theological training yet it is obvious that both were interiorly illumined by the Holy Spirit as they searched the
Scriptures, reflected on them, savoured them and then
put the word into practice in the humdrum circumstances of daily life. This young Carmelite, without
any particular theological training, but illumined by
the light of the Gospel, feels she is being taught by the
divine Teacher who, as she says, is 'the doctor of
Doctors', and from him she receives 'divine teachings'.[30]

When did this love of scripture begin for Thérèse?
If we read her autobiography and letters we glimpse
the attraction the word of God had for Thérèse from
an early age. In her childhood she had listened carefully to the scripture texts that she read within larger
books on the Christian life, *The Imitation of Christ* and
The Lives of the Saints. We know that within her own
family home there was a reading each evening from a
book called *The Liturgical Year* in which there were
many scripture texts from the liturgy.[31] These would
have nourished Thérèse on the sound teaching she
would later draw on when nothing else seemed to
speak to her heart. In fact she tells us that at one point
in her life, all books left her in a state of helplessness
and aridity.

> In this helplessness, Holy Scripture and the
> Imitation come to my aid; in them I discover a
> solid and pure nourishment. But it is especially
> the Gospels which sustain me during my hours
> of prayer, for in them I find what is necessary for
> my poor little soul. I am constantly discovering
> in them new lights, hidden and mysterious
> meanings'.[32]

Like Francis, Thérèse had a retentive memory and she could recite by heart, whole texts from scripture. These texts referred not only to those relating to her 'Little Way' but also to various texts, which she drew upon when teaching the novices. Her sister, Celine, (Sister Genevieve) recalls:

> Her excellent memory enabled her always to
> recall the best of whatever she had read or heard.
> In this way she found it easy to illustrate a point
> by a little anecdote or by some other shrewd
> observation. This was especially true in the field
> of Holy Scripture.[33]

Towards the end of her life, Thérèse, like Francis, liked to hear the Gospel of the day. On one occasion Thérèse asked her sister, Pauline, (Mother Agnes of Jesus) to read the Gospel to her. However, Pauline did not have her missal with her but simply told Thérèse what the Gospel was about, whereupon Thérèse repeated the whole text by heart.

We have already mentioned the way in which both Francis and Thérèse used Scripture by weaving certain texts from different places. We have already referred to Francis love of the Psalms, especially the Divine Office and the Office of the Passion. Thérèse too, loved the Psalms and the Divine Office. She did not know Latin and had to rely on snippets of the Psalms heard or read elsewhere. Her sister, Celine, remembered that Thérèse did not wish to distract any sister before going to Chapel for the Divine Office, and she always tried to be very attentive when praying the psalms. Thérèse said, 'I do not believe that anyone could possibly desire more than I to recite the Divine Office perfectly and without a mistake.'[34] This remark probably refers to correct pronunciation and ceremonial.

Just as Francis had opened the Scriptures for counsel, Thérèse also opened the Scriptures randomly to encounter the Lord, and to discover his will. There are several instances recorded that confirm this approach to scripture.[35] There was the occasion before her Profession when Thérèse was seized with a terrible feeling of anguish. Her anguish was caused by a deep darkness regarding God's love for her and also her vocation to Carmel. She confided these doubts and temptations to Mother Gonzague who responded by sending Thérèse a little note of reassurance and encouragement. However, Thérèse tells us that she still doubted because she thought that the note was prompted by human affection. It was then she felt within her an impulse to consult the Gospels. 'And, when I opened them at random, my attention was caught by a verse I had never noticed previously, "For he whom God has sent speaks the words of God; for God does not give the Spirit by measure."'[36] Thérèse received her answer and was at peace.

When Thérèse was asked to write her biography, she knelt and prayed before the statue of the Blessed Virgin Mary. 'Then opening the Holy Gospels my eyes fell upon these words: "And going up a mountain, he called to him men of his own choosing, and they came to him." This is the mystery of my vocation, my whole life.'[37]

THE
MYSTERY
OF MY
VOCATION

CALLED & CHOSEN

Random opening of the scriptures was not the only way Thérèse approached the word of God. She also read attentively and assiduously searched the Scriptures until her heart found the fulfilment of her desires.

Like Francis, it would seem that intuitively she already knew what she was looking for, and reading and searching became both revelation and confirmation. 'I take up Holy Scripture, then all seems luminous to me; a single word uncovers for my soul infinite horizons.'[38] We have already referred to Thérèse finding her call and personal vocation to be love within the heart of the Church. She discovered this revelation by opening the Scriptures to find some kind of answer. She continued reading without becoming discouraged, until she found a sentence that consoled her. So, Thérèse read and searched until her heart found rest in the word that was already planted within her heart. Recognition came through personal reading, persevering searching, and trust in her divine Teacher within. We can understand her heartfelt words: 'Show me the secrets hidden in the Gospels. Ah! That golden book is my dearest treasure'.[39]

Thérèse: The Word of Love

At the top of one of her poems, Thérèse wrote the following words of St Gertrude.

> My daughter, seek those words of mine which most exude love. Write them down, and then, keeping them preciously like relics, take care to reread them often. When a friend wishes to reawaken the original vigour of his affection in the heart of his friend, he tells him: 'Remember what you felt in your heart when I said such and such a word', or 'Do you remember your feelings at such a time, on such a day, in such a place?'... Be assured then that the most precious relics of mine on earth are my words of love, the words which have come from my most sweet Heart.[40]

47

It is obvious that when Thérèse approached scripture it was to find there words of love that would nourish, inspire, inform, interpret and confirm her in her vocation and mission. 'She had discovered that the deeper knowledge of God's word could come only through love'.[41] The emphasis was love, the unfolding of which we will revisit in a future chapter.

For Francis and Thérèse, the words of God led to the discovery of the Incarnate Word, Jesus Christ. Both discovered the poverty and humility, the love and the littleness revealed in the Person of Jesus. It was the human face and heart of God that captivated the hearts of Francis and Thérèse. The genius and originality with which they lived the Gospel message is their enduring, unique legacy, which never ceases to have a universal appeal and relevance with a freshness that merited both saints being described as 'new' with special reference to their biblical spirituality. In her autobiography, Thérèse explicitly stated that she wanted to seek out a means of going to heaven by a little way, a way that is very straight, very short, and totally new. This new way she found in the word of God.

In May 1925, in his Address to the pilgrims of Bayeux and Lisieux, Pope Pius XI referred to this newness, shining forth in the life and message of Thérèse: 'Her Little Way is beautiful, fruitful and safe. It is a way of peace and holiness—a new omen to the world: omen novum'.[42] The Church in every age recognises and proclaims the way in which the word of God continues to find a new face in the lives of her saints. Because 'every saint is like a ray of light streaming forth from the word of God',[43] the saints bring something new and fresh to our understanding and lived expression of the word of God.

Celano, the biographer of Francis, refers to this newness embodied in the life of Francis and his fraternity: 'Suddenly, there leapt upon the earth a new man, a new army quickly appeared; and the peoples marvelled at the signs of an apostolic newness'.[44] That the word has creative power when the believer responds is evidenced in the life of Francis and his followers. Eight centuries later, the Franciscan charism lives on, because each person appropriates the Gospel gift with creative fidelity, in the uniqueness of God's personal call. Only in this way is tradition preserved and newness assured.

Francis: Message and Mission in the Word of God

That Francis discovered his message and mission in the word of God, and was profoundly shaped by it, is beyond doubt. This was manifested in his initial 'This is what I want; this is what I seek; this is what I desire with all my heart'[45] to his confident conviction that 'No one showed me what I had to do, but the Most High Himself revealed to me that I should live according to the pattern of the Holy Gospel'.[46] Francis also knew that he had a message and a mission to share his particular understanding of the word with all the faithful. 'Because I am the servant of all, I am obliged to serve all and to administer the fragrant words of my Lord to them'.[47]

His love and reverence for the 'the most holy words of the Lord', and the ministers of the word, 'We must honour all theologians and those who minister the holy divine words and respect them as those who minister to us spirit and life'[48] led to a profound and penetrating understanding of the mystery of God in human flesh.

Jesus Christ the Word of God and the written words became one, and this penetration of the mystery led to his unique form of imitation in love and littleness, manifested in the humility of Bethlehem, the self-giving love of Calvary and Christ's continuing loving presence with us in the humble bread of the Eucharist. This living, loving, humble presence will be developed in subsequent chapters.

Thérèse: Message and Mission in the Word of God

Like Francis, the sacred words of Scripture and the Word made flesh in Jesus Christ became one for Thérèse. 'To keep Jesus' word—that is the sole condition of our happiness, the proof of our love for him. But what is this word? It seems to me that Jesus's word is Himself. Jesus, the Word, the Word of God!'.[49] What Thérèse profoundly sensed and understood, was the word made flesh in Jesus Christ, and the call to live by this same word of love, as the heart of biblical revelation. That the science of love would express itself through her Little Way unexpectedly caused a storm of glory and a lasting legacy, earning Thérèse a place among the saints who have a special charism of Gospel wisdom.

During her life Thérèse discovered 'new lights, hidden and mysterious meanings' and received from the divine Teacher that 'science of love' which she then expressed with particular originality in her writings. This science is the luminous expression of her knowledge of the mystery of the kingdom and of her personal experience of grace. It can be considered a special charism of Gospel wisdom which Thérèse, like other saints and teachers of faith, attained in prayer.[50]

In his Apostolic Exhortation, *Verbum Domini*, Pope Benedict expressed the desire 'that the Bible may not be simply a word from the past, but a living and timely word'.[51] Francis and Thérèse are examples of the way in which the word of God is living and timely. When this happens, not only are the people themselves changed and transformed, they also have a lasting effect and influence on the Church and the world. Though centuries apart and very different in their chosen vocations, Francis and Thérèse were kindred spirits and heralds of the Gospel in their own time and place, proclaiming the timeless and ever new Gospel message as a living and timely canticle of love. 'The word of God has bestowed upon us the divine life which transfigures the face of the earth, making all things new (cf. Rev 21:5). His word engages us not only as *hearers* of divine revelation, but also as its *heralds*'.[52] We will now explore the particular emphasis and originality that unite Francis and Thérèse, the troubadours of love and littleness, in their chosen way of following of Christ, as heralds of the Good News.

Reflection

The Word of God was central in the lives of Francis and Thérèse and shaped their vocation and mission in life. How important is the Word of God for you and how does it shape your life?

Notes

1 R. J. Armstrong, OFMCap., W. J. A. Hellmann OFM.Conv., W. J. Short, OFM. *Francis Of Assisi The Saint Early Documents*, vol. I, (London, New York: New City Press, 2000), p.125.

2 Carmel of Kilmacud, *Thoughts of the Servant of God Thérèse of the Child Jesus*, (P. J.Kenedy & Sons, USA: The Plimpton Press, 1914), p. 199.

3 T. Matura, OFM., *Francis of Assisi The Message in His Writings*, Trans. By P. Barratt, OFMCap., (USA: The Franciscan Institute, St Bonaventure University, 1997), p. 4.

4 R. J. Armstrong et al., *Francis Of Assisi The Saint*, vol. I, pp. 201–2.

5 R. J. Armstrong, OFMCap., W. J. A. Hellmann, OFMConv., W. J. Short, OFM., *Francis of Assisi The Founder Early Documents*, vol. II, (London, New York: New City Press, 2000), pp. 85–6.

6 *Ibid.*, p. 38.

7 R. J. Armstrong *et al.*, *Francis Of Assisi The Saint*, vol. I, p. 125.

8 Armstrong *et al.*, *Francis of Assisi The Founder,* vol. II, p. 631.

9 *Ibid.*, p. 643.

10 J. Clarke, OCD., (Trans.) *Story of a Soul: The Autobiography of St Thérèse of Lisieux*, (Washington D.C.: ICS Publication, 1976), p. 71.

11 *Ibid.*, p. 99.

12 *Ibid.*, pp. 193–4.

13 Armstrong *et al.*, *Francis Of Assisi The Saint*, vol. I, p. 132.

14 *Ibid.*, p. 125.

15 Saint Bonaventure, 'Letter in Response to an Unknown Master', *Works of St Bonaventure, Writings Concerning the Franciscan Order,* vol. 5, (USA: The Franciscan Institute, St Bonaventure University, 1994), p. 51.

16 Armstrong *et al.*, *Francis of Assisi The Founder,* vol. II, p. 314.

17 Armstrong *et al.*, *Francis Of Assisi The Saint,* vol. I, p. 202.

18 Pope Benedict XVI, *Spe Salvi,* 4.

19 Armstrong *et al.*, *Francis of Assisi The Founder,* vol. II, p. 314.

20 *Ibid.*, p. 613.

21 Armstrong *et al.*, *Francis of Assisi The Saint,* vol. I, p. 283.

22 *Ibid.*, p. 79.

23   *Ibid.,* p. 80.

24   Armstrong *et al., Francis of Assisi The Founder,* vol. II, p. 612.

25   B. Vollot, 'The Diatessaron and Earlier Rule of St Francis', in *Greyfriars Review,* 6/3, (USA: The Franciscan Institute, St Bonaventure University, 1992), pp. 279–317.

26   Armstrong *et al., Francis of Assisi The Founder,* vol. II, p. 316.

27   Armstrong *et al., Francis of Assisi The Saint,* vol. I, p. 126.

28   D. V. Monti, 'Do the Scriptures Make a Difference in our Lives?' *Franciscans and the Scriptures Living the Word of God,* Washington Theological Union Symposium Papers, (USA: The Franciscan Institute, St Bonaventure University, 2005), p. 12.

29   Pope John Paul II *Divini Amoris Scientia,* 1.

30   *Ibid.,* 7.

31   J. Bergstrom-Allen, & W. McGreal, (ed.) *The Gospel Sustains Me The Word of God in the Life and Love of Saint Thérèse of Lisieux,* (UK: St Albert Press & Rome: Edizioni Carmelitane, 2009), p. 24.

32   Clarke, *Story of a Soul,* p. 174.

33   C. Martin, (Sister Genevieve of the Holy Face), *A Memoir of my Sister St Thérèse.* (Dublin: MH.Gill and Son Limited, 1959), pp. 106–7.

34   *Ibid.,* p. 102.

35   H. U. von Balthasar, *Two Sisters in the Spirit, Thérèse of Lisieux and Elizabeth of the Trinity.* (San Francisco: Ignatius Press, 1992), pp. 85–6.

36   T. Taylor, Rev, *Saint Thérèse of Lisieux, The Little Flower of Jesus,* (London: Burns Oates & Washbourne Ltd., 1927), pp. 223–4.

37   Clarke, *Story of a Soul,* p. 13.

38   J. Clarke, OCD. *St Thérèse of Lisieux: General Correspondence,* vol. II. (Washington, D.C.:ICS Publications, 1988), Letter 226, p. 1094.

39   D. Kinney, O.C.D. *The Poetry of St Thérèse of Lisieux,* p. 126.

40   J. McCaffrey, OCD., *Captive Flames, A Biblical Reading of The Carmelite Saints,* (Ireland: Veritas Publications, 2005), p. 171.

41   *Ibid.,* p. 171.

42   Taylor, *Saint Thérèse of Lisieux,* p. 276.

43   Pope Benedict XVI, *Verbum Domini,* 48.

44   Armstrong *et al., Francis of Assisi The Founder,* vol. II, p. 399.

45   Armstrong *et al.*, *Francis of Assisi The Saint,* vol. I, p. 201.
46   *Ibid.,* p. 125.
47   *Ibid.,* p. 45.
48   *Ibid.,* p. 125.
49   Carmel of Kilmacud, *Thoughts of the Servant of God Thérèse of the Child Jesus,* p. 199.
50   Pope John Paul II, Divini Amoris Scientia, 1, 7.
51   Pope Benedict XVI, *Verbum Domini,* 5.
52   *Ibid.,* 91.

Chapter 3

The Infant Jesus

The most high Father made known from heaven through His holy angel Gabriel this Word of the Father — so worthy, so holy, and glorious — in the womb of the holy and glorious Virgin Mary, from whose womb He received the flesh of our humanity and frailty.[1]

St Francis

Sister Thérèse kept 25 March each year as a day of special devotion. It was the Feast of the Incarnation and, as she used to tell us, the Infant Jesus, in the bosom of Mary, was never as small as He was on that day.[2]

Celine/Sister Genevieve

T o speak of Francis and Thérèse and their particular way of following Christ, roots us in the Incarnation. The Word made flesh in the person of Jesus Christ was their central focus and inspiration for their spirituality of love and littleness. A God who humbled himself in becoming a baby in the womb of Mary, being born in a stable, living and growing to maturity within the normal limitations of the human condition in Nazareth and finally submitting to death on a cross, profoundly affected Francis and Thérèse. The way in which their lives witness to love and littleness has become a lasting legacy for the Church and the world, known respectively as Franciscan spirituality and Theresian spirituality.

Our interest in this book is the way in which both saints develop their way of relating to God with overlapping similarities, but with originality that also makes them distinct. This authenticates the presence of the Holy Spirit, who creatively brings to birth something new in the life of every person who responds to his or her personal and unique vocation. The Church in our day is calling for a renewed sense of vocation. In 1997 in a Pontifical Document entitled *New Vocations for a New Europe*, we read:

> The human being, in fact, is 'called' to life, and how one comes to life, carries and finds in itself the image of the One who calls. Vocation is the divine invitation to self-realization according to this image, and is unique-singular-unrepeatable precisely because this image is inexhaustible. Every creature expresses and is called to express a particular aspect of the thought of God. There each finds a personal name and identity; affirming and ensuring a unique freedom and originality.[3]

Pope Benedict, during his recent visit to England, expressed the same invitation by proclaiming the universal call to holiness, promoting a culture of vocation. Francis and Thérèse exemplify what is involved. They pave the way for a deeper understanding of personal vocation and response, after the example of God in human flesh with particular emphasis on the crib, the cross and the Eucharist. Let us now turn to Francis and his devotion to the Infant Jesus.

The Father's Gift, Mary's Son

Captivated by the humility of God becoming a human being in the womb of Mary, Francis understood the mystery of the Incarnation, first and foremost, as the outpouring of love within the Trinity. That God should assume our humanity and frailty, and identifying with us in every way, except sin, led Francis through contemplation, prayer and praise, to the imitation of Christ in poverty and humility, love and littleness.

Addressing and thanking God the Father who sends the Son and makes him known, Francis says: 'Through your holy love with which you loved us, You brought about his birth as true God and true man by the glorious, ever-virgin, most blessed, holy Mary'.[4] He repeats the gratitude and recognition of the great love of the Father in his *Salutation of the Blessed Virgin Mary*, describing his love for the Mother of God and the Father's gift of the Son through her. She, who is full of grace, conceives the only Son of the Father by the creative love of the Holy Spirit. The Franciscan theologian, Eric Doyle writes, 'From the Holy Spirit we have that tiny, vulnerable adorably attractive little child and that is God'.[5] Francis was overawed by the mystery of the extravagant love within the Trinity, revealed to us in the humanity of Jesus, born of the Virgin Mary.

> Hail, O Lady, Holy Queen,
> Mary, holy Mother of God,
> Who are the Virgin made Church,
> chosen by the most Holy Father in heaven
> whom he consecrated with his most holy beloved Son
> and with the Holy Spirit the Paraclete,
> in whom there was and is
> all fullness of grace and every good.[6]

In his personal writings, when speaking of the gift of Jesus, Francis intimately links the extravagant and humble love of the Father with the choice and vocation of Mary, the humble virgin. Penetrating the mystery of God as a human baby highlighted for Francis the unique role of Mary in conceiving and giving birth to God's own Son. With God as father and Mary as mother, what an awesome reality the Incarnation really is. As Eric Doyle, once remarked that the Incarnation is 'too fantastic to be false'.[7]

The Feast of Feasts

The God-man, who became a tiny baby thrilled the heart of Francis to such an extent that he referred to Christmas as the Feast of Feasts. This great feast led Francis into the heart of the Trinity, into the humility of God who chose to become little, dependent and limited, like every human person. The implications for our understanding of God are immense, regarding both his divinity and humanity and his chosen way of relating to us.

> He (Francis) used to observe the Nativity of the Child Jesus with an immense eagerness above

all other solemnities, affirming it was the Feast of Feasts, when God was made a little child and hung on human breasts. He would kiss the images of the baby's limbs thinking of hunger, and the melting compassion of his heart toward the child also made him stammer sweet words as babies do.[8]

What Francis did for the medieval world continues to be a breath-taking revelation for every age. Where God seemed distant, majestic and glorious, judging the world from his high throne in Heaven, it was the genius of Francis to make God accessible, lovable and approachable. Not only did Francis wish to speak about the humble God in a manger in Bethlehem, he wished to re-enact that scene with dramatic effect, and in so doing make present the mystery of God among us.

I wish to enact the memory of that babe who was born in Bethlehem: to see as much as is possible with my own bodily eyes the discomfort of his infant needs, how he lay in a manger, and how, with an ox and an ass standing by, he rested on hay.[9]

The humble cave in Greccio became the new Bethlehem. Francis awakened love for the Infant Jesus 'since in the hearts of many the child Jesus had been given over to oblivion. Now he is awakened and impressed on their loving memory by His own grace through His holy servant Francis'.[10] Francis will be forever associated with the Christmas crib, a tradition that continues to delight both young and old. However, the essence of this is not mere sentiment but deep theological and spiritual insight into the nature of God made man and the way in which he is present among us.

THE **FEAST** OF **FEASTS**

Significantly, Francis re-enacted the Bethlehem scene during the celebration of the Mass, clearly illustrating his understanding of the connection between Word and Sacrament. We will develop this relationship in a later chapter. Here we merely wish to point to the connection Francis made between the Incarnation and the Eucharist.

> Therefore: children, how long will you be hard of heart? Why do you not know the truth and believe in the Son of God? Behold, each day He humbles Himself as when He came from the royal throne into the Virgin's womb.[11]

One of the consequences of this amazing truth of God among us as a human being was the relationship it created between Jesus and Francis, a cherished relationship that would shape his life, his message and his mission to the world.

Jesus our Brother

In his second biography of Francis, Friar Celano tells us that Francis embraced the Mother of Jesus with inexpressible love, since she made the Lord of Majesty a brother to us.[12] A brother! Jesus as brother! How amazing! Out of the abundance of his grateful heart, Francis overflowed in words of wonder, praise and thanksgiving for such a brother: 'O how holy and how loving, gratifying, humbling, peace-giving, sweet, worthy of love, and above all things desirable it is to have such a Brother and such a Son: our Lord Jesus Christ'.[13]

This precious relationship of brother was central to Francis's understanding of the deep mystery of God with us. Not only did he regard every human person as a brother and sister; Francis also regarded every aspect of created reality as brother and sister.

The world became his cloister where he excluded no one and no thing, and all because of what happened in that humble manger in Bethlehem over two thousand years ago.

According to Eric Doyle, the most significant word in St Francis's life and writings is friar. It is a translation of the Latin word for brother. It was for him a primordial word, a word of mystery that told him something about everything. St Francis loved Jesus Christ as the First Brother of us all. This happened when Jesus was born just like us, little, dependent, frail and vulnerable. Francis could never forget such humility and condescension on God's part. 'Indeed, so thoroughly did the humility of the Incarnation and the charity of the Passion occupy his memory that he scarcely wanted to think of anything else.'[14] We have pointed out some of the main features of Francis's devotion to the Infant Jesus: humility, love, littleness, brotherhood and motherhood in relation to the Trinity, to Mary, to every human person, to the whole of creation in the context of the ordinariness of our daily living and loving. We will leave the last word to Francis:

> We are brothers to Him when we do the will of the Father who is in heaven. We are mothers when we carry Him in our heart and body through divine love and a pure and sincere conscience and give birth to Him through a holy activity which must shine as an example before others.[15]

Thérèse: Devotional Background

To understand the background for Thérèse's devotion to the Child Jesus, it may be helpful to mention the devotions associated with The Child of Prague and The Child Jesus of Ittenbach of Messina. At the time of Thérèse, it is probable that in every Carmel there was a statue of the Infant of Prague. This devotion dates back to 1600s and is associated with a Spanish noble-woman, Maria Manriques de Lara, who gave the statue to her daughter as a family heirloom when she married the Chancellor of Bohemia. Later the statue was given to the Carmelite monastery near Notre Dame des Victoires in France and the devotion spread throughout the world, popularised by the Carmelites. The small wax statue was clothed in gold and the Child Jesus held a globe in one hand while the other was raised in blessing. By resting the globe in Jesus's hand, the artist evokes the mastery that Christ exercises over the world: 'He is before all things and everything subsists in Him'. (Col 1:17), and 'In your hand are power and might' (1 Ch 29:12). Thérèse may have been thinking about this statue when she proclaimed in one of her poems:

> With the same little hand
> that caressed Mary
> You upheld the world
> and gave it life
> and you thought of me.[16]

Thérèse would have been familiar with this statue and devotion, possibly at home, where she had a rich devotional life, and certainly in Carmel, where the Christ Child was invoked under the title of the 'Divine Little Great One'. This image meant a lot to Thérèse and later would greatly influence her doctrine of The Little Way of Spiritual Childhood. We can still see the holy card kept by Thérèse, which has a conversation between Jesus and a child, in which Jesus tells the child that he accepts every sorrow—exile from heaven, pains, tears, and blasphemy, because of love. Thérèse paraphrases a saying of St Bernard that she freely quoted: 'Jesus, who made you so little?—Love'. The actual quote from St Bernard is: 'The greatest of all beings became the littlest. Who accomplished this wonder? Love!'[17] And Thérèse realised that Love was never smaller than at the moment of conception in the Virgin Mary's womb and this is why she kept the feast of The Annunciation as a day of special devotion.

The second image of the Child Jesus with which Thérèse was familiar was the Child Jesus from Itten-bach of Messina. Marie-Loiuse Castel, who was one of Thérèse's novices and became Sister Marie of The Trinity and of the Holy Face, brought this image from the Paris Carmel on Avenue Messina. Thérèse kept this picture with her until the end of her life. In 1897 she explained its significance by saying that in raising his right hand to heaven, Jesus seemed to be saying to her: 'You will come with me to Paradise, it is I who tell you so'.[18] Thérèse also had the task of decorating the 'pink' Child Jesus in the monastery cloisters, the one she saw smiling at her through the flowers and lights as she entered the snow-covered cloister garden on her Clothing Day. While Thérèse nurtured her devotional life in keeping with current practices associated with the Child Jesus, she was deeply rooted in the Word of God, which provided her with sound teaching and fresh insights relating to her cherished spirituality of childhood. This phase of development would emerge and mature during her years in Carmel. Prior to that, the Holy Spirit was paving the way through ordinary circumstances, popular devotions, and family relation-ships and through the hopes and dreams that are part and parcel of growing up.

Before Carmel

When Thérèse was just nine years old she was meditating on what name she would like when she entered
Carmel. She loved her own name, Thérèse, and wished
to keep it, but then she adds, 'All of a sudden, I thought
of Little Jesus whom I loved so much, and I said, Oh!
How happy I would be if they called me Thérèse of
the Child Jesus!'.[19] In a subsequent visit to Carmel,
Thérèse spoke to the Prioress, Mother Marie de
Gonzague, about her desire to be a Carmelite. The year
was 1882. A few weeks after her visit, the Prioress
actually proposed the name Sister Thérèse of the Child
Jesus. Thérèse had not mentioned this name to the
Prioress during their conversation and was therefore
amazed and overjoyed, saying that she considered it
a 'singular favour from my beloved Child Jesus'.[20]
Apparently, Mother Marie de Gonzague had suggested the name in memory of St Teresa of Avila's
niece, Teresita, who had entered Carmel at the age of
nine.

Before she entered Carmel, a second significant
event associated with her devotion to the Child Jesus
was what Thérèse refers to as her Christmas grace.
Almost fourteen, Thérèse described herself as unbear-
able because of her extreme touchiness and over-
sensitivity. She cried profusely and then cried because
she had cried. It seemed she was quite unable to
control her tears or correct this fault—as she refers to
it. However, she tells us that God would have to work
a miracle to cure her, and this he did on Christmas day.
Like Francis, Thérèse linked the Christmas mystery
with the mystery of The Blessed Trinity and the
mystery of Christ in the Mass. She tells us that on that
unforgettable night she had the happiness, of receiving

the strong and powerful God. The paradox is that the weak, frail, poor little Christ Child gave the weak, frail, poor little Thérèse the strength of a warrior. As a result of this encounter of human weakness with divine strength, Thérèse left behind her childhood ways forever. It was a decisive and momentous event in her life that marked a new stage on her journey to God.

> On that luminous night, which sheds such light on the delights of the Holy Trinity, Jesus, the gentle little Child of only one hour, changed the night of my soul into rays of light. On that night when He made Himself subject to weakness and suffering for love of me, He made me strong and courageous, arming me with His weapons. Since that night I have never been defeated in any combat, but rather walked from victory to victory, beginning, so to speak, 'to run as a giant'.[21]

This giant's course would eventually develop into the Little Way of Spiritual Childhood. Initially, Thérèse out of her own experience of weakness and inner poverty, identified with the poverty and humility of the Child in Bethlehem. Her penetrating grasp of the Incarnation from birth to death lies at the heart of Thérèse's teaching about her Gospel way to God. It led her to embrace her littleness with confidence and joy.

After Carmel

When Thérèse crossed the threshold of Carmel in April 1888, it was the transferred feast of the Annunciation, a feast she held dear because Jesus, in the bosom of Mary, was never as small as He was on that day. As previously suggested by the prioress, Mother Marie de Gonzague, Thérèse was called Sister Thérèse of the

Child Jesus. Humanly speaking, while leaving behind the ways of childhood, Thérèse of the Child Jesus would now embark on living a life based on the virtues of childhood: trust, surrender, abandonment, confidence and love. Her Little Way of Spiritual Childhood would take root in the desert of Carmel, founded and grounded in the Word of God.

Scriptural Foundations

Scripture became ever more important for Thérèse after her entrance into Carmel. Although she would not have had access to a full bible, she was very familiar with particular texts that highlighted God's love and mercy towards 'little ones'. These texts were gleaned from the Old Testament. Celine, her sister, brought with her, at her own entrance, a copybook in which she had written out many Old Testament extracts. These enlarged Thérèse's horizons considerably, especially concerning 'little ones', and she grew in her understanding of God caring as a mother, with herself as a 'little one'.

The Old Testament texts that especially attracted Thérèse and became the foundation for her Little Way were from the Book of Proverbs and the Prophet Isaiah, 'Whoever is a little one, let him come to me' (Pr 9:4), and wondering what God would do when the little one came to Him, Thérèse found her answer in the Prophet Isaiah 'As one whom a mother caresses, so I will comfort you; you shall be carried at the breasts, and upon the knees they shall caress you' (66:13, 12). Thérèse was overjoyed by the tenderness and mercy of God. She felt she had no need to grow up; rather she felt the call to remain little and become so more and more. This may sound like an easy path but as her Little Way unfolded and developed, it was an all-embracing way of love, reaching into the depths of what it means to be a contingent and intrinsically poor human being, yet possessing a divine spark that unites every human person with the Incarnate Word who, at his birth, became a brother to everyone.

Jesus as Brother

Thérèse, like Francis, needed a God in human flesh, one like herself in her frail humanity, whom she could call brother. Just as Francis re-enacted the Bethlehem scene at Greccio, Thérèse also acted out the Bethlehem scene with her sisters by writing a Christmas play for a paraliturgical celebration of Christ's birth. She called her play, 'The Divine Little Beggar of Christmas'. Thérèse, like Francis, was overawed by the love of the Divine and Omnipotent God, asking for the love of his creature in a state of dependence, humility and poverty.

Thérèse composed the verses of this play, which were then separated into single verses on separate sheets of folded paper and placed in a basket before the statue of the Child Jesus. Each sister would come forward, choose a folded paper, and then offer herself as a gift using the words Thérèse had already written. The verses referred to offering oneself to the Christ Child and different aspects of ordinary daily living were offered: a smile; a song; a mirror, reflecting his virtues; a palace, representing the dwelling place of the heart, and many more—fifteen verses in all. Thérèse's own folded paper was a verse about a bunch of grapes, representing the acceptance of suffering. This she must have taken quite seriously as a gift she could offer the Child Jesus, because later, in painting a personal coat of arms with the Child Jesus and the Holy Face, she divided the painting diagonally, connecting the birth and the passion by the vine.

In writing this Christmas play and involving her sisters, Thérèse, like Francis at Greccio, wanted to dramatize the Incarnation and portray the humility and poverty of the babe of Bethlehem.

> So, look at this poor stable; see
> (His glory He has veiled, from love)
> The Beggar-child of Christmas! He
> has left His palace up above.
> *You* poverty (I know) embrace;
> Your peace of heart is there.[22]

In several poems, Thérèse too, like Francis before her, rejoiced in the relationship she had with Jesus as a brother, 'God here, our little Brother made'.[23]

> My need: a heart that burns with tenderness,
> where—ever a support—my head can lay;
> that loving me—my frailty no less,
> the whole of me!—won't leave me, night or day! …
> I must have *God* to put on humankind—
> become my Brother, suffering for me.[24]

At first glance, both Thérèse and Francis may be misinterpreted as romantic and sentimental regarding their devotion to the Child Jesus: Francis and the dramatic re-enacting of the first Christmas night; Thérèse writing letters to the Infant in the Crib and strewing petals before her pink statue of the Child Jesus. Far from sentimentality, the spirituality and theology underlying both saints' devotion to the Child Jesus is rooted in the sound doctrine of the Incarnation and the implications and consequences for every human person. Neither

Francis nor Thérèse separated the mystery of the human birth of Jesus from the other mysteries of his life, passion, death and resurrection. In fact Thérèse, as we have already said, in painting a personal coat of arms divided the painting diagonally, connecting the birth and the passion by the vine. Francis, in associating the manger with the sacrifice of Calvary at Midnight Mass, clearly demonstrates that for him too Christmas and Easter are inseparable. There would be no Easter without Christmas.

GOD HERE OUR
LITTLE BROTHER
MADE

Francis and Thérèse: Virtues of Poverty and Humility

Francis and Thérèse realised that the babe born in Bethlehem was the only Son of the Eternal Father. As child of the Father, Jesus was always before the Father as one who receives totally and, as such, Jesus personifies poverty and humility. This is what Francis and Thérèse understood and embraced. As a result, they lived in confident trust and loving surrender because they realised that what they contemplated in the Child Jesus was relevant throughout the whole of life. One never ceases to be poor and humble, little and loving, dependent and trusting before God, whatever one's age or stage of development. Their lives bear witness to the truth spoken by Jesus, 'Unless you become like little children, you will never enter the Kingdom of Heaven. And so, the one who makes himself as little as this little child is the greatest in the kingdom of heaven' (Mt 18:3–4). We see here the positive choice and decision to become little—the one who *makes himself* as little as this little child—what a mystery lies here! There is a process that is freely chosen, a Gospel path that is rooted in the truth of our being. The prophet Job stated the obvious when he said: 'Naked I came from my mother's womb, naked I shall return again' (Jb 1:21). We are ontologically poor! This is what the Incarnation teaches us.

> Son of the Father from all eternity, Jesus did not cling to his equality with God, but in a moment in history, through the Incarnation, he became as we are: poor. Here we are speaking not of material poverty, but of intrinsic poverty, the fact that we are contingent beings, dependent on God for our very existence.[25]

Following the example of Jesus, Francis and Thérèse show us how to live this truth in the ordinary circumstances of our very ordinary lives. Just as God lay hidden in a poor little baby, so too God is embodied in the warp and woof of our human existence, in all its poverty and dependency. And yet, at the same time, because of God becoming flesh like us, we have a dignity and preciousness that makes us God-like.

> Consider, O human being, in what great excellence the Lord God has placed you, for He created and formed you to the image of His beloved Son according to the body, and to His likeness according to the Spirit.[26]

Francis: Poverty and Humility

Contemplating the child in the manger led Francis to a deep understanding of the love and goodness of God who chose to be poor to enrich us. This was the wonderful exchange that captivated his heart and led to imitation of the poor Christ. 'Though He was rich, He wished, together with the most Blessed Virgin, His mother, to choose poverty in the world beyond all else'.[27] Such an exchange of love led Francis to esteem 'Lady Poverty' above all.

Poverty was not an end in itself. Therefore, Francis not only embraced and understood the meaning of material poverty, he also understood that exterior, material poverty was a symbol and reflection of that inner poverty that God embraced when he assumed the human condition and became as we are. He emptied himself. He set his glory aside. He did not cling to his equality with God. He was limited in his humanity and recognised that everything is a gift from the Father. 'By myself I can do nothing' (Jn 5:30).

Gazing at the dependent child in Bethlehem led Francis to accept and rejoice in his own poverty before God. We really are truly poor in the sense that we are totally dependent on God who is the source of our life, our gifts, our talents, our accomplishments and our virtues because God alone is the 'fullness of good, all good, every good, the true and supreme good, Who alone is good'.[28] Therefore to become self-sufficient, and to appropriate any good to ourselves alone by exalting ourselves because of the good God works through us, either by word or deed, is vainglory. It is a denial of the truth about ourselves, in that we do not attribute to God the glory that belongs to Him. 'Let us refer all good to the Lord, God Almighty and Most High, acknowledge that every good is His, and thank Him, from Whom all good comes, for everything'.[29]

Recognising our intrinsic poverty, Francis clearly and frequently spelled out the implications and consequences for daily living and loving. And it was literally in the everyday, mundane circumstances of ordinary life and relationships that Francis affirmed the central place of 'Lady Poverty' in his own life and in the lives of his followers. Especially in his *Admonitions*,[30] Francis gives very practical examples of the way in which the Holy Spirit works in those who recognise their poverty before God, as opposed to those who act according to their own egocentric desires and motivations and seek their own exaltation and glory.

Francis must have known from personal experience the many and subtle ways the human heart expresses itself. The examples given in *The Admonitions* relate to everyday events and circumstances—pride, envy,

impatience, gossip, personal gifts, good looks, learning
… the list goes on—and they all fall under the umbrella
of the commandment of love, a theme we will return
to in a later chapter.

In many of his writings, Francis seems to speak of
poverty and humility in the same breath. 'Let all the
brothers strive to follow the humility and poverty of
our Lord Jesus Christ'.[31] Francis clearly outlines the
importance of each of these virtues and their purpose
in our daily lives. 'Lady holy Poverty, may the Lord
protect you, with Your Sister, holy Humility!. Holy
Poverty confounds the desire for riches, greed, and the
cares of this world. Holy humility confounds pride'.[32]
So closely related are these two virtues that we can
associate both with the very beginning of the life of the
Christ Child in Bethlehem, in the awesome revelation
of the poverty and humility of God. It is truly amazing
that Francis grasped the meaning of poverty and
humility within the Trinity by contemplating the poor
and humble Christ in the crib. It is also truly amazing
that his contemplation of the Christ Child led him to
a profound understanding of the dignity of the human
person, made in God's image.

Towards the end of his life, Francis in his prayer,
The Praises of God, acclaimed: 'You are humility'.[33]
Christ did indeed humble himself and become poor as
we are. He not only suffered the privation of a stable
birth and refugee status, he also let go his divinity and
assumed the lowly guise of a creature, a real limited
human being. This realisation led Francis to a profound sense of his own poverty before God, and his
humble stance among his brothers and sisters. Consequently, he identified with the lowly, with the minores
of his day, those without power, prestige, wealth and

status. If this was the path Christ took, then Francis, his most perfect disciple, would do likewise.

Thérèse: Poverty and Humility

We have already observed that self-chosen material poverty is a reflection of inner poverty of spirit. Thérèse, like Francis, was used to a comfortable life-style at home. Even when she entered Carmel, Thérèse recalls, 'During my postulate I was pleased to have for my use, anything that was nice, and to find at hand whatever was necessary'.[34] Gradually, with the help of God's grace, Thérèse became detached from the material things that naturally delighted her. She gives the instance of having a lantern, much needed for her work, which another sister must have taken by mistake. Thérèse was left without the necessary means of light, but instead of bewailing her loss she came to the conclusion that poverty consists in being deprived not only of things desirable, but of those also that are indispensable. With this realisation, she grew in her desire for external poverty, and on one occasion she was delighted when another sister walked off with her pretty little jug and left in its stead a large ugly chipped one. These are small things, maybe, but they are concrete, everyday examples of a personal choice for material poverty.

In her poem, 'The Divine Little Beggar-Boy of Christmas', Thérèse seems very much aware of the poverty and deprivation of the Christ Child, and she refers to different aspects of this poverty in the poem. In one verse it is the deprivation of the stable as opposed to the riches of heaven. 'This stable! Jesus, looking, sees nothing to joy His heart. ... So, look at this poor stable; see (His glory He has veiled, from love) The Beggar-child of Christmas'.[35] In another verse, Thérèse speaks of the poverty of hunger. 'Since poverty is now so near: Sister, a drop of milk to feed Jesus, your little Brother here!.'[36]

The diocesan tribunal, which was set up in 1910, interviewed forty witnesses who testified to the holiness of Thérèse.[37] Poverty was one of the virtues commented upon by the witnesses. They referred to everyday, mundane situations where Thérèse practised the virtue to a heroic degree. The examples included instances when Thérèse was overlooked in the refectory. The sister in the refectory forgot to serve her and she simply went without her food and did not draw attention to the oversight. There were other occasions when the sister who sat next to her took almost everything for herself and gave no thought to the needs of Thérèse. Again, Thérèse accepted the situation without complaint and simply identified with the poor who are often in need and deprived of necessary sustenance.

The poor Christ Child was dressed in swaddling clothes and laid in a manger. For love of him Thérèse chose the poorest clothes, and she even asked Sister John the Baptist, who was in charge of the linen room, to give her the most worn and the oldest veils. This sister also said that the slippers Thérèse wore had to be burned after her death. They were so worn out and mended that no other sister could wear them. Many other instances were given relating to Thérèse's love for poverty.

Like Francis, Thérèse was careful about appropriating anything or anyone. During the Process of Beatification, Thérèse's sister, Celine, (Sr. Genevieve) said,

> To sum up these ideas on poverty, here is one piece of advice she gave me towards the end of her life: I had expressed the desire that a certain picture she had would come to me after her death. 'So, you still have desires!'. She said. 'When I am with God, don't ask for anything I had; just take what you are given. To behave any other way would mean that you were not stripped of everything.'[38]

It was obvious that when Thérèse gazed on the child in the crib, she was moved by the love that prompted such all-embracing self-emptying. Imitation was love's response.

Over time, Thérèse matured in her understanding of poverty and was led to a much deeper understanding and expression of it. She moved from exterior detachment to interior detachment and, like Francis before her, detached herself from all vainglory in acknowledging the truth about personal gifts, talents and inspirations. In humility, she recognised that all good and all glory belong to God.

> I should find no difficulty in never reclaiming them when they are sometimes taken away from me. The goods of heaven don't belong to me either; Dear Mother, I was writing yesterday that since earthly goods do not they are *lent* to me by God, who can withdraw them without my having a right to complain.[39]

Towards the end of her life when she was lovingly cared for in her illness, she admitted that she did not feel the pinch of poverty because she did not lack anything. Thérèse appreciated all the love and attention given to her, yet she could also write, 'This affection is very sweet to me. This is why I dream of a monastery where I shall be unknown, where I would suffer from poverty, the lack of affection, and finally, the exile of the heart'.[40]

Every witness at the Beatification Process also attested to the humility practised by Thérèse in the ordinary circumstances of life in Carmel. Examples abound. Her sister, Pauline, (Mother Agnes of Jesus) testified that even in her childhood Thérèse was grounded in humility, having been trained by a deep, disciplined love that neither spoiled nor flattered her. Interestingly, Thérèse herself admits that she was not indifferent to praise in her early years and she even thanked God when something happened to counterbalance the praise she sometimes received. Her self-knowledge and her keen insight into, and observation of, human nature enabled her to recognise the wilfulness of the human heart.

Mother Agnes of Jesus recalled that Thérèse once told her that Our Lord showed her that true wisdom consisted in desiring to be ignored. She took this very seriously and on the day of her Profession she carried a note next to her heart, saying, 'May nobody take any notice of me; may I be trodden underfoot like a grain of sand'.[41] This prayer was certainly granted as the following few examples show. According to Sister Mary Magdalen of the The Blessed Sacrament, there was the occasion when a sister saw Thérèse approaching and she said, 'Look at the walk of her! She's not in any hurry. When is she going to start working? She's good for nothing'.[42] Thérèse overheard these remarks and when she met the sister concerned, she gave her a big smile and did not harbour any hurt or bitterness towards her.

Another witness, Sister Teresa of St Augustine, recalled Thérèse sharing with her several conversations with sisters during her last days in the Infirmary. There was the Sister who came to visit Thérèse and said, 'If only you knew how little you are liked or appreciated!'. There was another Sister whom Thérèse overheard, saying, 'I don't know why they talk so much about Sister Thérèse; she doesn't do anything remarkable. We never see her practising virtue; in fact she could hardly be called even a good religious!'. And what was Thérèse's response to these comments? Sister Augustine recalled Thérèse's words, 'Oh, just imagine hearing that I was not a good religious, just when I am on my deathbed. What joy! Nothing could have given me greater pleasure'.[43] Such a response may seem strange to us, unless we grasp Thérèse's blend of realism and idealism in living a life in conformity with the Word Incarnate. Her perceptive knowledge of the struggle within the human heart, led her to weigh everything in the light and truth of eternity. Thérèse knew that she was the recipient of the extravagant love and goodness of God. Like Jesus, child of the Father and her brother, she too received everything from the Father. On her deathbed Thérèse said: 'Yes, it seems I never looked for anything but the truth; yes, I have understood humility of heart. It seems that I am humble'.[44]

Francis and Thérèse: The Centrality of the Incarnation

Francis and Thérèse are saints of the Incarnation. Their understanding of the Christ mystery places them within the prophetic tradition of the Church. Both show us how to live the Incarnation with particular emphasis on the poverty, humility and patient suffering expressed in the birth, and continued in the life, death, resurrection and continuing humble presence of God among us. The birth of Jesus did not stand apart from the rest of his life, as he identified and lived within the limitations of the human condition to the very end. As one theologian writes:

> The Incarnation is this movement of descent; it is not a static situation that ends in the passion and death. Therefore, in the mind of Francis, the passion is intimately linked to the birth. And so we should not be surprised to find that in Franciscan portrayals of the nativity, the shadow of the cross appears on the horizon.[45]

It is well documented that when Thérèse contemplated the Child Jesus in the crib, he was not separated from the mystery of Calvary.[46] In the collection of holy pictures that Thérèse was familiar with, there were several depicting the child in the crib with the cross in the background. Sometimes Jesus was represented as holding the cross or the crown of thorns. Christians of the nineteenth century were familiar with depictions like these. The French school of spirituality saw the yes of the incarnate Jesus from womb to tomb. Thérèse, in painting her own coat of arms, sketched the face of the Child Jesus in the crib on one half of the canvas, and the sorrowful face of Jesus during his passion on the other.

Having explored, to some extent, the great devotion of Francis and Thérèse to the birth of Jesus, especially in relation to poverty and humility, we will now move into the mystery of the cross and the way in which Francis and Thérèse understood and embraced this mystery in their own lives.

Reflection

When you contemplate God in human flesh, what new insights, challenges and invitations move your heart, especially in relation to poverty and humility?

Notes

1 R. J. Armstrong, OFMCap, W. J. A. Hellmann, OFMConv., W. J. Short, OFM., *Francis of Assisi The Saint. Early Documents,* vol. I, (London, New York: New City Press, 2000),p. 46.

2 C. Martin, (Sister Genevieve of the Holy Face), *A Memoir of My Sister St Thérèse.* (Dublin: M.H.Gill and Son Limited, 1959), p. 46.

3 Pontifical Work for Ecclesiastical Vocations, *In Verbo tuo,* 13.

4 Armstrong *et al., Francis of Assisi The Saint,* vol. I, p. 82.

5 J. Raischl, SFO, & A. Cirino, OFM, *My Heart's Quest Collected Writings of Eric Doyle Friar Minor Theologian,* (Canterbury, England: Franciscan International Study Centre, 2005), p. 19.

6 Armstrong *et al., Francis of Assisi The Saint,* vol. I, p. 163.

7 Raischl, & Cirino, *My Heart's Quest,* p. 158.

8 R. J. Armstrong, OFMCap, W. J. A. Hellmann, OFMConv, W. J. Short, OFM, *Francis of Assisi The Founder Early Documents,* vol. II, (London, New York: New City Press, 2000), p. 374.

9 Armstrong *et al., Francis of Assisi The Saint,* vol. I, p. 255.

10 *Ibid.,* p. 256.

11 *Ibid.,* p. 129.

12 Armstrong *et al., Francis of Assisi The Founder,* vol. II, p. 374.

13 Armstrong *et al., Francis of Assisi The Saint,* vol. I, p. 49.

14 *Ibid.,* p. 254.

15 *Ibid.,* p. 42.

16 P. Descouvemont (Text) H. N. Loose (Photographs) *Thérèse and Lisieux.* (Canada: Novalis, MI: Eerdmans, Dublin: Veritas, 1996), p. 135.

17 *Ibid.,* p.134.

18 *Ibid.,* p. 205.

19 J. Clarke OCD, (Trans.) *Story of a Soul: The Autobiography of St Thérèse of Lisieux,* (Washington D.C.: ICS Publication, 1976), p. 71.

20 *Ibid.*, p. 71.
21 *Ibid.*, p. 97.
22 A. Bancroft, *St Thérèse of Lisieux Poems*, p. 99.
23 *Ibid.*, p. 98.
24 *Ibid.*, p. 75.
25 P. Jordan, FSM., *An Affair of the Heart A Biblical and Franciscan Journey*, (Herefordshire: Gracewing, 2008), p. 26.
26 Armstrong *et al.*, *Francis of Assisi The Saint*, vol. I, p. 131.
27 *Ibid.*, p. 46.
28 *Ibid.*, p. 85.
29 *Ibid.*, p. 76.
30 *Ibid.*, pp. 128–137.
31 *Ibid.*, p. 70.
32 *Ibid.*, pp. 164–5.
33 *Ibid.*, p. 109.
34 Thérèse of the Child Jesus, *Thoughts of the Servant of God Thérèse of the Child Jesus*, Translated from the French by an Irish Carmelite, (New York: P. J. Kenedy & Sons, 1915), p. 97.
35 Bancroft, *St Thérèse of Lisieux Poems*, pp. 93, 99.
36 *Ibid.*, p. 94.
37 C. O'Mahony, *St Thérèse of Lisieux by those who knew her Testimonies from the Process of Beatification*, (Dublin: Veritas, 1975).
38 *Ibid.*, p. 148.
39 J. Clarke, *Story of a Soul*, p. 233.
40 *Ibid.*, pp. 217–8.
41 O' Mahony, *St Thérèse of Lisieux by those who knew her Testimonies from the Process of Beatification*, p. 59.
42 *Ibid.*, p. 264.
43 *Ibid.*, p. 197.
44 Clarke, *Story of a Soul*, p. 270.
45 N. Nguyen-Van-Khanh, OFM, *The Teacher of His Heart Jesus Christ in the Thought and Writings of St Francis*, Translated by Ed Hagman, OFMCap, (New York: The Franciscan Institute, 1994), pp. 109–110.
46 P. Descouvemont (Text) H. N. Loose (Photographs) *Thérèse and Lisieux*, pp. 156–157.

Chapter 4

The Suffering Servant

Indeed, so thoroughly did the humility of the Incarnation and the charity of the Passion occupy his memory that he scarcely wanted to think of anything else.[1]

Thomas of Celano

Beneath Your infant steps, I'll live while here below, in mystery:
I'll soften, too, Your steps—Your last ones, those that go to Calvary![2]

St Thérèse

In his humanity, Jesus, the revelation of the poverty and humility of God, was the model, example and inspiration for the chosen way of Francis and Thérèse. The poverty and humility they contemplated in the manger in Bethlehem continued to captivate their hearts, and forge in them the likeness of the Christ-form in littleness and love. Both of them understood the link and continuity between the birth, life and death of Christ. The life of God revealed in the humanity of Christ, immersed them in the mystery of suffering love.

Love and suffering are inseparable. Life begins with the birth pangs of labour. 'I shall give you intense pain in childbearing, you will give birth to your children in pain' (Gn 3:16). Life continues with the growing pains of childhood and adolescence. 'My child, why have you done this to us? See how worried your father and I have been, looking for you'. He replied, "Why were you looking for me? Did you not know I must be in my Father's house?" But they did not understand what he meant' (Lk 2:48–50). Life matures and becomes ever more fruitful in self-giving love, losing one's life for the sake of the other. 'No one can have greater love than to lay down his life for his friends' (Jn 15:13). Truly we are in the realm of mystery here, because suffering and love are woven into the fabric of the human condition. It was like this for Jesus. It was like this for Francis. It was like this for Thérèse, and this would seem to be the pattern for every human life. The question is: how do we make sense of this pattern of suffering and love?

Francis and Thérèse entered the mystery of suffering love by contemplating the life of God in the humanity of Jesus. They understood the love of the

Father who emptied himself in giving us the gift of the Son by the power of the Holy Spirit, thus revealing poverty and humility at the very heart of the Godhead. They understood the love of the Son in becoming as we are in all our human weakness and frailty, with the exception of sin. 'For the high priest we have is not incapable of feeling our weaknesses with us, but has been put to the test in exactly the same way as ourselves, apart from sin' (Heb 4:16).

Poverty, humility and patient suffering marked the life of the Son of God in increasing depth and intensity, culminating in his death on the cross. 'During his life on earth, he offered up prayer and entreaty, with loud cries and with tears' (Heb 5: 7).

In entering into the mystery of the Incarnation, Francis and Thérèse grew in their understanding of God and themselves. Ever the realists, both were keenly aware of their poverty before God and their need for a humble stance in the midst of their brothers and sisters, and indeed before the whole of creation. There is a depth of understanding hidden beneath the following statement of Francis, 'What a person is before God, that he is and no more',[3] and of Thérèse, 'I am really only what *He* thinks I am'.[4] Let us now turn to these two saints and learn from them, as we try to penetrate the mystery of suffering love as part and parcel of the human condition.

Francis and The Crucified Christ

At the very beginning of his conversion, it was the crucified Christ that melted the heart of Francis. St Bonaventure, in his biography of Francis, recalls that Francis sought out solitary places for prayer and meditation. On one such occasion when Francis was absorbed in prayer, 'Jesus Christ appeared to him fastened to a cross. His soul melted at the sight, and the memory of Christ's passion was so impressed on the innermost recesses of his heart'.[5] This sensitivity to the suffering of Jesus deepened and intensified with time. Somehow, it was the mystery of the crucified Christ that penetrated the consciousness of Francis so that, from the moment of his conversion, he was particularly attentive to suffering and its meaning in human life.

Friar Celano, the first biographer of Francis, draws our attention to the prayer of Francis in a little broken down Church of San Damiano. Again, it was the encounter with the crucified Christ that moved Francis towards deeper conversion of heart, so that he not only saw the crucified on the cross but he recognised Him in his suffering brothers and sisters. Sensitivity to the mystery of the suffering Christ empowered Francis to undertake a life of poverty and humility with all the suffering that such identification involved. He started where we all have to start, in the here and now of our everyday lives. Francis began by reaching out to lepers, even though the sight of them had previously nauseated him and he had gazed on them only from a great distance. Why this change in Francis? St Bonaventure tells us the reason. 'But now, because of Christ crucified, who according to the text of the prophet appeared despised as a leper, he, in order to despise himself completely, showed deeds of humility and humanity to lepers'.[6]

REACHING OUT TO LEPERS

This was a turning point in the life of Francis, because from that moment onwards, he recognised in the suffering bodies of his brother lepers the poor, humiliated and suffering Christ. This impacted his life so much that he made service to his brother lepers a requirement of his Gospel living, and he inserted this requirement into his written Rule of life for himself and his brothers. 'They must rejoice when they live among people considered of little value and looked down upon, among the poor and the powerless, the sick and the lepers, and the beggars by the wayside'.[7] In recognising the inviolable dignity of every human person, Francis lived in a fraternal relationship of equality with everyone. In choosing this particular stance of minority, that is, being a little brother to all, Francis knew that it would affect every aspect of life, especially those who touch our lives on a daily basis. This was not an easy option for Francis and the brothers, nor is it an easy option for any sincere disciple of the crucified Christ.

Francis and The Suffering Servant

The example of Christ coming among us in poverty and humility, and lovingly embracing the suffering involved in human living and loving, fired the heart of Francis to imitation and identification. Repeatedly he would advise his brothers and sisters to follow in the footsteps of our Lord Jesus Christ. 'The Lord's sheep followed him in tribulation and persecution, in shame and hunger, in weakness and temptation and in other ways'.[8] I wonder what Francis meant by these 'other ways'? Is he leaving each one of us the privilege of recognising our own path of bearing the cross, a way that is uniquely ours, for he once said, 'I have done what is mine; may Christ teach you what is yours'.[9]

Francis's heightened awareness of the suffering inherent in the human condition was profoundly affected by the way in which he gazed on the suffering servant of God, Jesus the Christ. 'Always he gazed upon the face of his Christ. Always he caressed the Man of Sorrows, familiar with suffering.'[10] There is great tenderness expressed here in the words Celano uses to describe Francis's relationship with God. We can sense the compassion in the heart of Francis, especially as he tenderly caressed the poor and humble God in Jesus Christ. So deeply had the passion of Christ imprinted itself on his heart, that he caused great concern to others when he was heard crying loudly and wailing as he walked in the woods around the Portiuncula. When approached and asked about his loud crying and wailing, Francis replied, 'I should go through the whole world this way, without any shame, crying and bewailing the Passion of my Lord'.[11]

Prayerful contemplation of the life of Christ in the poverty, humility and patient suffering of his hidden and public life, but especially in his all-embracing acceptance of death on a cross, filled Francis with wonder and awe, praise and thanksgiving and an exquisite sensitivity to all kinds of suffering. His compassionate heart was forged in the furnace of his own sufferings both interior and exterior as he contemplated Jesus, the suffering servant of God. Truly Francis realised that 'Ours were the sufferings he was bearing, ours the sorrows he was carrying' (Is 53:4), and Francis, like Jesus, endured and embraced his humanity and the humanity of others in the day to day living out of the Gospel of love, carrying those sufferings in his own body.

During thirty years in Nazareth, Jesus, the Son of God, lived a poor, obedient and hidden life. How awesome is that! Nobody was aware that the humble carpenter at his work bench in Nazareth was the second person of the Blessed Trinity, God in their midst, with a human face and a human heart. It is truly amazing that Jesus lived in obscurity, unknown and unrecognised for so long. Such an example did not escape the attention of Francis. Knowing how Christ lived, Francis was forever admonishing, advising and encouraging his brothers and sisters to follow the example of the Son of God, especially in his poverty and humility. Therefore, Francis did not want to draw attention to himself in any way that would bolster his ego and feed his need for public acclaim and vainglory.

The heart of Francis was purified and enlightened in his day to day living with the brothers. This was the crucible where Francis learned the real meaning of poverty, humility and suffering. His *Admonitions* spell out the reality of living a life of imitation of Christ. These *Admonitions* have been described in many ways, including *The Franciscan Sermon on the Mount*, *The Canticle of Minority*, and *The Magna Carta of Christian Brotherhood*, because these sayings of Francis reveal a way of life that is based on the Suffering Servant image in the practical and challenging circumstances of ordinary life. To this end, Francis is at pains to draw attention to the contrast between the spirit of the flesh and the Holy Spirit of God. In nearly all of the *Admonitions*, Francis refers to poverty, humility and patient suffering, and this is one reason why the *Admonitions* are called *The Canticle of Minority*. Life lived in the spirit of poverty and humility, with all the inevitable suffering this involves, becomes a song, a canticle, in loving imitation of Jesus, the Suffering Servant of God.

To follow in the steps of the Suffering Servant then, is to accept, embrace and bear the personal cross of what it means to be both a graced and sinful created being. It will engage us in recognising and accepting both blessedness and brokenness in ourselves and in others. Of necessity this will entail facing the meaning and reality of the cross in our everyday lives. This is what Francis faced, embraced and cherished. 'All the striving of this man of God, whether in private or in public, revolved around the cross of the Lord'.[12] It is worthwhile pondering the very profound and perceptive teaching of Francis as it translates into every day life, because his understanding of human nature is deeply penetrating and practical. With conviction he shares with us those moments in life where sin and grace battle for supremacy, but not without interior and exterior suffering. Perhaps in his telling the story of true joy, Francis illustrates the extent to which he suffered and triumphed amidst poverty, humiliation and rejection.

The story about true joy is recognised as a precious teaching that Francis learned possibly from bitter experience. There are two different versions of the story. We will concentrate on the older version and rely on the insights drawn from that story over the years by Franciscan scholars.[13] The story goes that Francis outlines for brother Leo many success stories within the Order, all of which relate to growth and expansion, high-ranking prelates, archbishops and learned men, together with amazing feats in evangelisation and the working of miracles. Surprisingly, Francis maintains that true joy is not to be found in all these success stories. All of these things, while good in themselves, have the potential to give us a false sense of identity because it is very easy to glory in our personal gifts and successes, without acknowledging that everything comes from God. Instead, Francis believes that true joy consists in bearing patiently the cross of exile, rejection, misunderstanding and misjudgement without losing patience and peace. In this patient acceptance of suffering and the experience of poverty and humility that it entails, without becoming upset about it, lies true joy.

In the story of true joy, Francis gives the example of returning to his friary, cold, and hungry, muddy and wounded, only to be told that he is not wanted. Even when he reveals who he is, the reply is: 'Go away! You are a simple and stupid person! Don't come back to us again! There are so many of us here that we have no need of you'.[14] Poignant words indeed! It is possible that the story reflects the suffering Francis endured towards the end of his life, when the Order he founded deflected from his original vision of minority, of remaining small in every way, thus identifying with the 'little ones' in the Gospel. In time, he felt he had to resign as Minister General of the Order he had founded. The question remains: did he choose to go or was he pushed? Judging from Francis's own words in both his *Admonitions* and his story of *True Joy*, we may well wonder what really happened at that General Chapter. It is interesting that when Francis was describing the life of a Lesser Brother, he gives the example of what might take place during a Chapter.

> I would not consider myself a Lesser brother unless I had the attitude which I will describe to you. And he said: 'Here I am, a prelate of the brothers, and I go to the Chapter. I preach to the brothers and admonish them, and in the end they speak against me': "An uneducated and despicable man is not right for us; we do not want you to rule over us. You cannot speak; you are simple and ignorant"'.[15]

Out of love for the crucified Christ and all the sufferings he endured for love of us, Francis knew that suffering touches every human life, but because of Christ it is possible for us to respond in love, and to experience deep inner peace and true joy even in the midst of these things.

Francis knew that in his suffering, especially those sufferings he endured from those who were near and dear to him, he was one with Jesus, who was also mistreated, misunderstood, misjudged and rejected by the people he too had loved and served. Francis knew he must remain faithful to the One who had shown him the way from the very beginning. Leadership was taken from him, but fidelity to his crucified Lord by following in his footprints was his preferred way of teaching and preaching. He would again choose this path of personal example when he stepped down from his more prominent leadership role, saying to the brothers:

> Nevertheless, until the day of my death, I will continue to teach my brothers by my example and my life how to walk the road the Lord showed me and which I in turn showed them, so they have no excuse before the Lord.[16]

Francis still had lessons to learn regarding his own living out of the radical poverty and humility of the crucified Christ. Although he accepted the loss of leadership, he still grieved over some of the brothers who were giving bad example and had ceased following the path he had taught them. At this point, the Lord spoke to him in prayer: 'Why are you so upset, little man? Have I set you up as shepherd over my religion so that you can forget that I am its main protector?'[17] Was this a stern reprimand or a playful tease, reminding Francis that the Order itself did not belong to him? Every one and every thing had to be returned to God. In imitation of the crucified Christ, there was no place for self-appropriation.

> Though he was the originator and patriarch,
> he did not deem likeness to other Founders something
> to cling to.
> Rather, he emptied himself out
> and kept the attitude of a Minor,
> considering himself the servant of the rest of the friars.
> He admitted his ignoble and unlearned status,
> and thus it was that he humbled himself,
> obediently accepting even the death of his primitive
> ideal, which was *his* death on the Cross!
> Because of this God highly exalted him in the Church
> and bestowed on Francis the name of being
> 'The Saint most like Christ'.[18]

From his own painful growth in self-knowledge gained through the experience of living in fraternity, and through personal prayer, including times of darkness and spiritual crisis, Francis detected the movements of the different spirits that mobilise us into action, then as now. The Gospel message he proclaimed is timeless. His mission is universal and he knew it, and it is within the particular context of littleness and love, expressed in the choice of imitating the radical poverty and humility of the suffering Christ that the legacy of Francis continues.

> Listen, sons of the Lord and my brothers, pay attention to my words. Incline the ear of your heart and obey the voice of the Son of God. Observe His commands with your whole heart and fulfil His counsels with a perfect mind. Give praise to Him because he is good; exalt Him by your deeds; for this reason He has sent

you into the whole world: that you may bear witness to His voice in word and deed and bring everyone to know that there is no one who is all-powerful except Him.[19]

Francis learned from the example of the Son of God. Every age and stage of the historical life of Jesus revealed to Francis the loving tenderness of God's self-emptying, extravagant love. Not only the poverty, humility and suffering of the birth and hidden life impressed Francis, he also followed in the footsteps of Christ in his public ministry. Homelessness, hunger, misunderstanding, misjudgement, opposition, tiredness, rejection, betrayal and eventual death by crucifixion were part of the human journey of the Son of God. Even at the end of his life, Francis was still seeking to enter ever more deeply into the mystery of suffering love in perfect imitation of Jesus, so much so that in his long retreat on Mount La Verna, he prayed the following heartfelt and daring prayer.

> O my Lord Jesus Christ, two graces do I ask thee to grant unto me before I die: the first, that while I live I may feel in my body and in my soul, so far as is possible, that sorrow, sweet Lord, that thou didst suffer in the hour of thy most bitter passion; the second that I may feel in my heart, as far as may be possible, that exceeding love wherewith, O Son of God, thou wast enkindled to endure willingly for us sinners agony so great.[20]

Such a powerful prayer was answered in a most extraordinary and unexpected way. Francis had a vision of the crucified Christ in the form of a seraph and in that experience he was pierced through in his human flesh with the wounds of Jesus in his hands, feet and side. This was indeed the climax in his journey of loving identification with the crucified Christ. Francis and Christ were one in love and suffering because as Blessed John Paul II states, 'Human suffering has reached its culmination in the Passion of Christ. And at the same time it has entered into a completely new dimension and a new order: it has been linked to love.'[21] Francis became what he loved. He was totally transformed into the image of Jesus, bearing in his own mortal body the wounds of love that united him with the God of love, in whose image he was created from all eternity.

Thérèse and The Suffering Servant

Suffering was Thérèse's companion from the early days of her life. Just two weeks into her short life she suffered from intestinal troubles, to be followed shortly afterwards by more serious concerns for her very life. Just two months after her birth her mother wrote, 'She is very bad and I have no hope whatsoever of saving her. The poor little thing suffers horribly since yesterday. It breaks your heart to see her'.[22] Thérèse did recover but not without the trauma of leaving her beloved parents and family and going to the country to be brought back to health by a nurse called Rose Taille. When Thérèse eventually returned to her family as a healthy child, it was not long before deep psychological and emotional suffering etched itself on her young life once again. We have already referred to the death of her mother and how this impacted on Thérèse when she was four and a half. When she looked back to that time she said, 'I don't recall having cried very much, neither did I speak to anyone about the feelings I experienced. I looked and listened in silence'.[23] Later she suffered miserably and with great sadness during her school days at the Benedictine Abbey, but she realised that she had to persevere in spite of her sadness. Thérèse said that she did not have enough virtue to rise above the miseries she suffered at that time. We can assume that these were very distressing years for her sensitive nature.

Unlike Francis of Assisi whose early life was care-free and worldly, the young life of Thérèse was marked by interior suffering in a most profound way. When she became aware that her dearest sister, Pauline, was going to enter Carmel and leave her orphaned once again, Thérèse, in deep anguish of heart realised the pain of life.

> In one instant, I understood what life was; until then, I had never seen it so sad; but it appeared to me in all its reality, and I saw it was nothing but a continual suffering and separation. I shed bitter tears because I did not yet understand the joy of sacrifice'.[24]

What a comforting admission for us. Thérèse, like us, had to grow in her understanding of psychological and emotional suffering and its place and meaning in human life. Later in life she would write in one of her poems: 'Every creature can forsake me. Near you I'll know how to do without them without complaining'.[25]

From the age of nine Thérèse firmly decided that some day she would enter Carmel and this she wished to do at the age of fifteen. However, her wishes were thwarted because fifteen was considered too young for entry into the Lisieux Carmel. Other Carmels did not have this age limit necessarily (Marie of the Trinity, Thérèse's novice, had entered the Paris Carmel at sixteen) but the ecclesiastical superior (a priest, not the

Prioress who supported Thérèse) was currently stipu-
lating twenty one for entrance, having had a distressing experience with a former young novice. Therefore,
Thérèse endured further suffering and disappoint-
ments from her ecclesiastical superiors, Bishops and
even the Pope himself who did not immediately grant
her the permission she sought. Eventually when
permission was granted, Thérèse was very realistic
about the sufferings she would likely endure in
Carmel. She admits that she had no illusions about the
life ahead of her.

> Illusions, God gave me the grace not to have a
> single one when entering Carmel. I found the
> religious life to be exactly as I had imagined it,
> no sacrifice astonished me and yet, as you
> know, dear Mother, my first steps met with
> more thorns than roses! Yes, suffering opened
> wide it's arms to me and I threw myself into
> them with love.[26]

Thérèse was able eventually to embrace the sufferings
that came to her because she matured in love. In the
process of maturing, however, she had much to endure
and grapple with as she struggled to find her particular
way to union with her suffering Lord. It is interesting
that in her writings there are over four hundred
references to trials and sufferings. Obviously she, like
us, tried to make sense of her experiences in the light
of grace and in the mirror of the human life of Jesus,
but in her early years Thérèse admits that she was far
from being mature. Some of her sufferings, especially
towards the end of her life when she was diagnosed
with tuberculosis, were acute physical sufferings. Like
Francis, most of her sufferings were interior and often
unknown to all except herself.

Like Francis in his story of *True Joy*, Thérèse too knew from experience the meaning of suffering in living closely with others. These sufferings included misunderstandings, misjudgements, rejection, jealousy, cold, hunger and excruciating physical sickness. In addition, she suffered severe spiritual trials through aridity and temptations against faith, truly a dark night of the soul which lasted for a year and a half at the end of her short life.

From what we have intimated, it is obvious that Thérèse experienced many hardships in Carmel, not least of which were those inflicted by those with whom she lived, both professed sisters and novices. How did she cope? In the early years when she first entered the Convent, Thérèse endured the sufferings that came to her with fortitude, but over time Thérèse would learn to unite all her sufferings with Jesus, the Suffering Servant of God, and this union would eventually lead her to find joy even in the midst of great suffering. But this did not happen all at once. It was a gradual process and there are key events that show how Thérèse suffered, the effects the suffering had on her, and how she eventually came through the suffering to greater personal maturity and holiness.

The occasion of her mother's death, the separation from Pauline when the latter entered Carmel, and her father's mental illness, were three of the most intense periods of psychological suffering for Thérèse. We know that she became a changed child from the moment of her mother's death. From being an outgoing, affectionate, cheerful, vibrant and at times mischievous little girl, Thérèse became withdrawn, over-sensitive, touchy, timid, vulnerable and sad. She tried really hard to overcome the perceived weaknesses in her personality and in this she was determined and persevering, yet to no avail, except that it strengthened her character through on-going effort. It would take a miracle of grace for her to change. She refers to this phase of her childhood, between the ages of four and a half to fourteen, as the most painful. But Thérèse learned a very valuable lesson in all of this. Remaining little before God and trusting in Him with childlike confidence and love, paved the way for a spirituality that was uniquely hers. In a moment the Child Jesus cured Thérèse in a way that her efforts of ten years had not achieved. Jesus took the initiative and Thérèse knew it.

Thérèse admitted that Pauline's departure for Carmel broke her heart. She recalled it as a day of tears and blessings. Thérèse remembered looking at the blue sky and wondering how the sun could shine amid such sadness. Hers was an affectionate heart; she felt this separation very severely and was unable to deal with the emotional turmoil it caused within her. She acknowledged that the sufferings that preceded Pauline's entrance were nothing in comparison with those that followed. Frequent headaches, tearfulness, tiredness and insomnia were taking their toll on Thérèse. Eventually she collapsed. Her frail body could not bear the strain and stress. The trial was beyond her strength. Her subsequent illness seemed life threatening and for three months she lay at death's door, unable to recognise or communicate with the members of her own family. Fever, loss of appetite, delirium, hallucinations, paralysis and at times involuntary movements of her body were some of the symptoms she suffered from. The illness lasted from March until May, a long time for her family to watch and wait as they prayed unceasingly for her recovery. Thérèse later wrote: 'I was suffering very much from this forced and inexplicable struggle'.[27] This time, the Blessed Virgin took the initiative. It seemed to Thérèse that Our Lady's statue that was nearby came alive and Mary, her mother in Heaven, smiled on her. In that moment Thérèse was healed.

Some might say that hers was a psychosomatic illness but Thérèse and her family were convinced otherwise. 'I believe the devil had received an external power over me but was not allowed to approach my soul nor my mind except to inspire me with very great fears of certain things'.[28] In his Apostolic Letter *Salvifici Doloris*, Blessed John Paul II said:

> In the midst of what constitutes the psycholog-ical form of suffering there is always an experience of evil, which causes the individual to suffer … One cannot deny that moral suffer-ings have a "physical" or somatic element, and that they are often reflected in the state of the entire organism.[29]

This would seem to confirm Thérèse's own experience and her later insight into this episode of suffering in her life. Her sister, Celine, witnessed not only the illness, but also the ecstasy and the miraculous and instantaneous cure. Celine recalled terrifying scenes during Thérèse's illness which, she said, baffled medical science at the time. Like Thérèse, Celine was convinced that the devil had a hand in it. The theolo-gian Hans Urs von Balthasar seems to agree that this strange illness, which defied diagnosis, was a sort of mystical trial, the cure of which was a heavenly intervention. 'It was her first great vision and anyone who tries to psychologise it away has to contradict the saint's own unambiguous testimony'.[30] These two instances of intense suffering in the childhood of Thérèse relate directly to the loss of two mother figures in her life. It seemed fitting, therefore, that the Mother of all Mothers, the Blessed Virgin herself, should be the one to visit Thérèse and smile on her with tender, healing motherly love.

A third event in the childhood of Thérèse associated with her beloved father was also the occasion of both suffering and grace. It is interesting that once again it is through a parent figure that God chose to reveal his plan and entrust a special mission to Thérèse. It happened when Thérèse was about six or seven years old. Her father was on a business trip to Alençon when Thérèse had a vision of him in the garden at Lisieux, a vision that was so real that she cried out to him to get his attention. She described her father as much more stooped than usual, and his head was covered with a sort of apron which hid his face. At first, Thérèse thought her father was playing games with her but when the garden was searched her father was not there. She said the vision lasted but an instant, but it was so deeply engraved on her heart that fifteen years later it was as present as if it was actually happening. Thérèse was told to forget all about this incident but she couldn't. She even tried to make sense of it but she couldn't do that either; so she kept it at the bottom of her heart convinced that some day she would understand. And she did.

The vision Thérèse had of her stooped father with veiled face took on a meaning and reality that she would not have been able to bear as a child. She said that God parcels out sufferings and trials according to the strength he gives us and she adds, 'Never, as I've said already, would I have been able to bear even the thought of the bitter pains the future held in store for me. I wasn't even able to think of Papa dying without trembling'.[31] It was years later when Thérèse had already entered Carmel that she would understand the meaning of her childhood vision, becoming for her a central aspect of her spirituality, linking her forever with the devotion to The Holy Face.

Devotion to The Holy Face

Thérèse was nurtured in a family steeped in the devotional life of the Church at that time and one of the most popular was devotion to The Holy Face. This devotion originated with the picture of the suffering face of Christ, which was purported imprinted on the veil with which Veronica wiped the face of Jesus on his journey to Calvary. His Holy face was said to have appeared miraculously on the cloth and this became a precious relic in the early Church. All devotions wax and wane according to circumstances, individual charisms and the needs of the Church and the world and there was an upsurge in this devotion in the eighteen hundreds, mainly due to the revelations received by a holy Carmelite nun, Sister Marie of Saint Peter in the Carmel of Tours, and for four years Our Lord appeared to her and asked her to establish this devotion worldwide. The main purpose of the devotion was to make reparation for the sins of the world and to obtain favours from God.

Shortly after the death of Sister Marie of Saint Peter, Pope Pius IX ordered public prayers be offered in all churches in Rome to implore God's mercy on the Papal States due to a revolution occurring at the time. As part of these public prayers, a three-day exposition of the supposed relic of the Veronica's veil was held for public veneration at St Peter's Basilica. On the third day of the showing, a miracle occurred through which Our Lord's face on the veil became very distinct and glowed with a soft light. The Canons of the Basilica ordered the bells rung at sight of the miracle, which attracted crowds of people. The miracle lasted for three hours, and was attested to by an apostolic notary during the incident. That same evening etchings and representations of the effigy were made and touched to the original relic and later sent abroad. Afterwards, a custom was introduced where copies of the veil were sent to Rome to be touched to the original, making them objects of special devotion. These copies are typically noted to have stamps and/or wax authenticating seals in the lower corner, and they became relics which nurtured the devotion of the faithful, especially a certain Monsieur Dupont from Tours who had two of these relics in his possession. He hung one of these images in his home and had an oil lamp burning before it as a sign of his veneration and devotion. Miracles happened and devotion to the holy Face spread.

While devotion to the Holy Face of Jesus has always existed in some form or another, the revelations to Sister Marie of Saint Peter and the miraculous occurrences led to Pope Leo XIII establishing an Archconfraternity for the whole world. The Martin family, in touch with the thinking of the Church, immersed themselves in this devotion. On 26 April 1885, Thérèse, along with her father, Celine, Marie and Leonie, were enrolled in the Atoning Confraternity of the Holy Face. Thérèse was aware that the Holy Face was disfigured by blasphemy, insult and outrage, and she was part of a movement called to make reparation. Monsieur Guerin, Thérèse's uncle, had a reproduction of the picture of the Holy Face placed in St Peter's Cathedral in Lisieux, and he was personally responsible for the expense of keeping a lamp burning perpetually before the image.

Mother Genevieve of Saint Teresa, the revered foundress of the Lisieux Carmel, was a devotee and encouraged the sisters to adopt the devotion to the Holy Face. Therefore, Thérèse was on familiar devotional ground when she entered Carmel, and she credits Pauline with her deeper understanding of the Holy Face. For Thérèse the Holy Face was so much the symbol and expression of Jesus's love, unrecognised by many. New depths of meaning would unfold as she entered more deeply into this devotion. Specific aspects of humility and hiddeness were emphasised in the monastery as these resonated with the particular lifestyle and spirituality of Carmel. Thérèse was very impressed by all of this and she grew in her appreciation of it. When she received the habit of Carmel she added the title 'of the Holy Face' to her religious name, thereby she became known as Sister Thérèse of the Child Jesus of The Holy Face. For the rest of her life, Thérèse carried on her person a relic of the holy Carmelite nun, Sister Marie of Saint Peter of Tours, and a small picture of the Holy Face with her short prayer, 'Jesus, make me like You'. Like Francis on La Verna, praying to be identified with his crucified Lord, and never anticipating the consequences of his answered prayer, so too Thérèse could not have anticipated the depths to which this prayer of identification would lead.

Towards the end of her life when Thérèse was in private conversation with Sister Marie of the Sacred Heart, she recalled the strange vision of her father, which we have already mentioned. She writes, 'All of a sudden, while I was describing the details of the strange scene, we understood simultaneously what it meant'.[32] The simultaneous recognition was the connection between their father's illness and his identification with the suffering face of Jesus. Thérèse realised that just as the adorable face of Jesus was veiled during His Passion, so the face of their father had to be veiled in the days of his suffering from cerebral paralysis, in imitation of his suffering Lord. Thérèse referred to her father's mental illness as the family's greatest trial. Perhaps she suffered more than her sisters during this period because of the gossip that surrounded her father's illness, linking his state of health to Thérèse's leaving him and entering Carmel.

Thérèse like Francis, took to heart and understood from bitter experience, the words of the prophet Isaiah: 'He had no form or charm to attract us, no beauty to win our hearts, he was despised, the lowest of men, a man of sorrows, familiar with suffering, one from whom, as it were, we averted our gaze, despised, for whom we had no regard.'(Is 53:2–3). Francis saw the image of the Suffering Servant in his brother leper; Thérèse saw the image of the Suffering Servant in her own dear father. With this depth of faith and insight, Thérèse encouraged her sisters to see this ordeal as a family sharing in the Passion of Jesus. She referred to his illness as 'our great richness', and Celine recalled that it was Thérèse, the youngest member of the family who, with invincible acceptance of God's will, supported her older sisters during their very painful trial.

Thérèse said, 'Jesus must love our father dearly if he has to suffer like this'.[33]

Family and Carmelite devotion, as well as insightful and graced understanding of her everyday experiences, nurtured Thérèse's devotion to the Holy Face. Although she understood that the devotion was primarily associated with making reparation, Thérèse also focused on the merciful, tender love of God for all his children. Coupled with her love for the Sacred Heart, she understood that 'If the heart of Jesus is the symbol of love, his adorable face is its eloquent expression'. Those words were on a holy card Thérèse gave to one of the sisters in her community.

The sufferings of Thérèse were not only psychological. She also suffered from scruples, a most painful interior spiritual trial. This severe trial made her anxious and fearful of offending God because her love for Him was so intense. She could find no relief on earth from such moral suffering, so she turned to her little brothers and sisters who had died in infancy asking them to intercede for her, and her cross was lifted. This happened to her in childhood but Thérèse also seems to have had less severe bouts of scruples throughout her life. She had to be firmly reassured by a Confessor that she had never committed a mortal sin. Apparently when a handwriting analyst studied some of Thérèse's writing in Carmel, he described her as very impressionable, weak, fearful and overly sensitive but with an iron will and boundless energy. Therefore, there was possibly a residue of fear and scrupulosity in Thérèse, even in Carmel. In addition to her occasional scrupulosity and ongoing aridity in prayer, Thérèse suffered a most severe spiritual darkness during the last eighteen months of her life. She referred to it as 'eating at the table of sinners'. Prior to that time she had experienced a living faith and immense joy at the thought of Heaven where she would meet God face to face. She could hardly understand how anyone could doubt the reality of life after death. However, that reality changed for Thérèse when she was plunged into severe darkness, a real trial of faith for her.

Joyful, living faith was changed into an experience of dense fog, a searing trial and temptation against faith. Even the thought of heaven caused bitter torment and struggle within her. This suffering was so intense that Thérèse said a person would have to actually travel through this dark tunnel to understand the thick darkness in which she was engulfed. She shared with her sister Pauline that she had horrible thoughts, which constantly oppressed her, but she felt she must endure this suffering, caught up as she was in doubt and near despair, eating the bread of sorrow on behalf of her unbelieving brothers and sisters. This was her participation in the passion of Christ. She expressed what she was going through by using images and comparisons, but her trial of faith was so great that Thérèse felt she could not share deeply about it. 'I fear I might blaspheme; I fear even that I have said too much'.[34] Such a harrowing experience reduced Thérèse to the brink of desolation, but in her pain and isolation, deprived of the joy of faith, Thérèse embraced the will of God with the determination to believe what she knew deep down to be true, without the felt knowledge of previous years. From Thérèse's own words, we get a glimpse of the intensity of her physical and spiritual sufferings during the last months of her life, 'No, I would never have believed that it was possible to suffer so much ... never, never. I can only explain it by my extreme desire to save souls'.[35] Without doubt, Thérèse looked upon her sufferings as a share in the redemptive sufferings of Christ. As Blessed John Paul II writes:

> For it is above all a call. It is a vocation. Christ does not explain in the abstract the reasons for suffering, but before all else he says: "Follow me!". Come! Take part through your suffering in this work of saving the world, a salvation achieved through my suffering!'[36]

SHARING
CHRIST'S
SUFFERING

Francis and Thérèse: Singers of a New Song

While in the lives of both Francis and Thérèse, we see evidence of psychological, spiritual and physical sufferings taking their toll on their frail bodies, we also witness the emergence of a canticle of love and integration at the very point where suffering reaches a climax in their lives. Francis and his Canticle of Creatures, written at the end of his life when he was in the utmost state of poverty, pain and suffering of body and soul, and ends his canticle with a wonderful invitation: 'Praise and bless my Lord and give Him thanks. And serve Him with great humility.[37] Thérèse in her Canticle of Merciful Love, that is her autobiography, and in some of her poems, written when she too was in a state of utter weakness of body and profound darkness of soul, could eloquently sing: 'In peace, sweet Jesus, I want to wait for Your return, without ever ceasing my canticles of love.[38]

How is it possible to sing a canticle of love to the Lord in such circumstances? By following in the footsteps of the Incarnate Christ, the Suffering Servant of God, both Francis and Thérèse matured through various stages of revulsion and acceptance of suffering, until they finally reached a stage of embracing suffering with joy because love transformed them into living images of the One who bears the wounds of suffering love in his glorious, risen body, Jesus the Christ. In fact both of them passed beyond even the desire to suffer in union with Christ. Their one and only longing was to be united with Jesus, whether in salvific suffering or in risen joy, because everything is but a means towards total union with the crucified and risen Jesus.

The question now is: what can we learn from Francis and Thérèse when we are faced with the inevitable sufferings that are part and parcel of human life, because as Blessed John Paul II says,

> In whatever form, suffering seems to be, and is, almost inseparable from our earthly existence. … Suffering belongs to human transcendence: it is one of those points in which we are in a certain sense 'destined' to go beyond ourselves, and we are called to this in a mysterious way.[39]

Speaking of the reality of transcendence in the experience of the stigmata, the climax of Francis's identification with his crucified Lord, a contemporary author speaks of the lesson we can learn from this. 'Francis experienced the immanence of God in his flesh. The lesson of the stigmata is that the Incarnation is not only a divine event that broke through history but also a human possibility that can break through our lives'.[40] That Christ continues to live in us and through us is indeed the most profound mystery, and when deeply entered into gives meaning to every detail of our lives, including the great mystery of suffering, which seems to be inseparable from self-giving love.

It is interesting that while Francis bore the sacred stigmata in his flesh in a visible way during his earthly life, Thérèse, sought to have those wounds (hidden while she was on earth) shining in her glorified body: 'I hope in heaven to resemble You and to see shining in my glorified body, the sacred stigmata of Your Passion'.[41] That same wounded and risen Jesus Christ, beloved of Francis and Thérèse, remains with us, and will remain with us until the end of time, in poverty, humility and self-sacrificing love as our Bread of Life in the mystery of his Eucharistic presence, which is the theme of our next chapter.

Reflection

Has the example of Francis and Thérèse in any way changed your understanding of the place of suffering, and its meaning, in your life and in your image of God and your relationship with Him?

Notes

1   R. J. Armstrong, OFMCap, W. J. A. Hellmann, OFMConv, W. J. Short, OFM., *Francis of Assisi The Saint Early Documents,* vol. I, (London, New York: New City Press, 2000),p. 254.

2   A. Bancroft, (Trans) *St Thérèse of Lisieux Poems,* (London: Fount, Harper Collins, 1996), p. 165.

3   Armstrong *et al., Francis of Assisi The Saint,* vol. I, p. 135.

4   C. Martin, (Sister Genevieve of the Holy Face), *A Memoir of my Sister St Thérèse,* (Dublin: MH.Gill and Son Limited, 1959), p. 202.

5   R. J. Armstrong, OFMCap, W. J .A. Hellmann, OFMConv, W. J. Short, OFM, *Francis of Assisi The Founder Early Documents,* vol. II, (London, New York: New City Press, 2000), p. 534.

6   *Ibid.,* p. 534.

7   Armstrong *et al., Francis of Assisi The Saint,* vol. I, p. 70.

8   *Ibid.,* p. 131.

9   Armstrong *et al., Francis of Assisi The Founder,* vol. II, p. 386.

10   *Ibid.,* p. 303.

11   *Ibid.,* p. 180.

12   *Ibid.,* p. 401.

13   A. Jansen, OFM, 'The Story of the True Joy: An Autobiographical Reading', in *Greyfriars Review,* 5/3, (USA: St Bonaventure University, 1991), pp. 367–387.

14   *Ibid.,* p. 368.

15   Armstrong, *et al., Francis of Assisi The Founder,* vol. II, p. 341.

16   Jansen, 'The Story of the True Joy: An Autobiographical Reading', p. 381.

17   Armstrong *et al., Francis of Assisi The Founder,* vol. II, p. 349.

18   A. W. Romb, 'The Franciscan Experience of Kenosis', in *The*

Cord, 41/5, (USA: St Bonaventure University, 1981), pp. 145–155.

19   Armstrong *et al., Francis of Assisi The Saint,* vol. I, pp. 116–7.

20   M. A. Habig, (Ed) 'Third Consideration on the Sacred Stigmata', *St Francis of Assisi. Writings and Early Biographies,* (USA: Franciscan Herald Press, 1983), p. 1448.

21   Pope John Paul II, *Salvifici Doloris,* 18.

22   J. Clarke, OCD, (Trans.) *Story of a Soul: The Autobiography of St Thérèse of Lisieux,* (Washington D.C.: ICS Publication, 1976), p. 6.

23   *Ibid.,* p. 33.

24   *Ibid.,* p. 58.

25   D. Kinney, OCD, *The Poetry of Saint Thérèse of Lisieux,* (Washington DC: ICS Publications, 1996), p. 207.

26   J. Clarke, *Story of a Soul,* p. 149.

27   *Ibid.,* p. 65.

28   *Ibid.,* p. 63.

29   Pope John Paul II, *Salvifici Doloris,* 6,7.

30   H. U. von Balthasar, *Two Sisters in the Spirit Thérèse of Lisieux and Elizabeth of the Trinity,* (San Francisco: Ignatius Press, 1992), p. 98.

31   Clarke, *Story of a Soul,* pp. 47–8.

32   *Ibid.,* p. 47.

33   C. O'Mahony, *St Thérèse of Lisieux by those who knew her, Testimonies from the Process of Beatification,* (Dublin: Veritas, 1975), p. 141.

34   Clarke, *Story of a Soul,* p. 213.

35   C. Martin, *A Memoir of my Sister St Thérèse,* p. 239.

36   Pope John Paul II, *Salvifici Doloris,* 26.

37   Armstrong *et al., Francis of Assisi The Saint,* vol. I, p. 114.

38   Kinney, OCD,*The Poetry of Saint Thérèse of Lisieux,* p. 208.

39   Pope John Paul II, *Salvifici Doloris,* 2.

40   G. T. Straub, *The Sun and Moon over Assisi A Personal Encounter with Francis and Clare,* (Cincinnati, Ohio: St Anthony Messenger Press, 2000), p. 260.

41   Clarke, *Story of a Soul,* p. 277.

Chapter 5

The Bread of Life

O sublime humility! O humble sublimity! The Lord of the universe, God and the Son of God, so humbles Himself that for our salvation He hides Himself under an ordinary piece of bread![1]

St Francis

Hidden as a Wafer here, You live for me: Jesus, for You I'll also hide away![2]

St Thérèse

At the beginning of this chapter we take to heart those words of Blessed John Paul II when he spoke of placing ourselves 'at the school of the saints, who are the great interpreters of true Eucharistic piety. In them the theology of the Eucharist takes on all the splendour of a lived reality; it becomes contagious and, in a manner of speaking, it warms our hearts'.[3] Francis and Thérèse belong to this school, and their lives and writings proclaim their profound understanding of the Eucharist as the manifestation of the humble love of God remaining with us as *'the gift par excellence*, for it is the gift of himself, of his person in his sacred humanity'.[4] This sacred mystery is central for Francis and Thérèse as they develop their relationship with the Incarnate Christ in His total self-giving love. Such amazing love, made manifest in the humble and hidden form of ordinary bread and wine, captivated the hearts of Francis and Thérèse in the same way that the Babe of Bethlehem and the Suffering Servant touched their innermost being, and made present for them the vulnerability of a love and littleness that holds nothing back.

Though steeped in the traditional teaching and piety of the Church, Francis and Thérèse were not constrained within the narrow confines of some of the thinking of their contemporaries. They brought to their times an approach to and understanding of the Eucharist that touched hearts anew with an authenticity and originality that continues to teach, inspire, inflame and encourage true devotion to the Real Presence of the Person of Christ in the Eucharist. To see Francis and Thérèse in the context of their own times may help us to appreciate the tremendous contribution they made to the developing understanding and appreciation of the Eucharist as the logical continuation of the Incarnation and Redemption.

Francis and The Eucharist in The Middle Ages

It is well documented that from the sixth century onwards there was a decline in devotion to the Eucharist. By the time Francis came on the scene in the twelfth century this decline had reached crisis point, and the Fathers of the Fourth Lateran Council in 1215 had to address this crisis and remind both clerics and lay people about their obligations. The Council Fathers were aware that the faithful were no longer receiving Our Lord in the Eucharist and even the Priests were failing to celebrate Mass more than four times a year and, in the intervening time, did not even attend Mass. Rather than receive the Eucharist, people tended to venerate and adore the Real Presence, especially after the Consecration. This practice developed because it was during this period that the Elevation of the Host after the Consecration was introduced and, while this led to external devotion, the reception of the Sacrament declined. Obviously there were many factors that contributed to this moral and religious impasse.[5]

It is generally agreed by historians that Francis was present at the Fourth Lateran Council, and his writings demonstrate that he took to heart the concerns of the Council Fathers. Following on from the Lateran Council, Francis may also have been familiar with and influenced by a Eucharistic Letter, *Sane cum olim*, written in November 1219 by Pope Honorius III. In this letter, the Pope strictly enjoined that the Eucharist should be reserved and adored with great respect, reverence, honour, care and cleanliness. From such detailed instructions it is obvious that there was a lack in these areas, and the Writings of Francis pick up on these very issues.

In addition to the external realities that had to be addressed, Francis was also passionately concerned with the intimacy of the person-to-person encounter with Christ that the Eucharist made possible. Therefore, rather than use the word Eucharist, Francis repeatedly uses the phrase the Body and Blood of the Lord. This down to earth, Incarnational language directly links the mystery of the Eucharist with the mystery of the birth of Jesus who came in flesh and blood like ours, and with the shedding of His blood on the Cross. We shall see later in this Chapter, the way in which Francis addressed issues of abuse, neglect, indifference and heresy regarding the Eucharist, which were rampant at that time.

Thérèse and The Eucharist in the Nineteenth Century

Turning now to Thérèse, we cannot fully understand her contemporary situation and attitude to the Eucharist without some awareness of the effects of the French Revolution. During that time (1789–1799) Catholics were persecuted and there was overt hostility to Christian worship, therefore many forms of piety, including Eucharistic devotion fell into decline. However, in nineteenth-century France, Thérèse was part of a culture where devotion to the Blessed Sacrament experienced a revival and her faith-filled family participated wholeheartedly in this liturgical revival. Holy men and women, founders of Religious Orders and saints of that era, made Eucharistic devotion and adoration the centre of their spirituality. Notable among these are the names of the Venerable Leo Dupont, (whom we have already met in relation to the devotion to the Holy Face), Saint John Mary Vianney, Saint Julian Eymard and many others who introduced new Eucharistic devotions such as The Forty Hours Adoration. We know that Thérèse participated in this devotion in Carmel, and her poetry reveals the depth of her Eucharistic meditations during those hours, a theme we shall return to later.

France led the way in nurturing devotion to the Eucharist. For instance, the first informal Eucharistic Congress took place in France in 1874 followed by a formal, organized Eucharistic Congress in Lille, France in 1881, approved by Pope Leo XIII. Later in 1905, Pope Pius X presided over a Eucharistic Congress in Rome. Over time this practice spread and continues to the present day, with a Eucharistic Congress in Dublin, Ireland in June 2012. Centuries before, Francis acknowledged that Thérèse's homeland was more special than other regions because of their love for the Body and Blood of the Lord and, because of this, Francis wished to live and die there. He said to the brothers:

> In the name of our Lord Jesus Christ, of his glorious Virgin Mother and of all the saints, I choose the region of France, in which there is a Catholic people, especially because of the other Catholics of the holy Church. They show great reverence to the Body of Christ, which pleases me very much. Because of this, I will gladly live among them.[6]

In the school of the saints devoted to the Eucharist (already referred to) Francis and Thérèse grace us with their particular insights and emphasis on humility, with far-reaching implications and consequences for each one of us. A number of Francis's Letters are referred to as Eucharistic Letters and a number of Thérèse's Poems are likewise devoted to this subject.

Francis: Bethlehem and The Eucharist

A recurring theme in the writings of Francis is the humility of God. This is particularly apparent when Francis writes about the Body and Blood of the Lord in the Eucharist. 'The Lord of the universe, God and the Son of God, so humbles Himself that for our salvation He hides Himself under an ordinary piece of bread! Brothers, look at the humility of God'.[7] What captivates the heart of Francis is the reality of the Real Presence of the Lord Jesus Christ in the silent, hidden and humble form of bread and wine, offering Himself as our spiritual food and drink. Bread is the staple diet of many people, particularly the poor who do not have access to the choice and variety of their richer brothers and sisters. And this is the form in which the omnipotent God chose to remain with us. It is an awesome mystery indeed! And so Francis prays, 'Give us this day our daily Bread: Your own beloved Son, our Lord Jesus Christ'.[8]

Francis readily makes the link between Bethlehem, the 'House of Bread', with the Living and life-giving Bread of the Eucharist.

> Behold, each day He humbles Himself as when He came from the royal throne into the Virgin's womb; each day He comes to us, appearing humbly; each day He comes down from the bosom of the Father upon the altar in the hands of priest.[9]

This profound understanding of the mystery of the
Incarnation and the Eucharist is emphasised by Francis
to defend the truth in the face of the Cathar heresy,
which denied the reality of the Incarnation. Cathar
error held that matter was evil; therefore a Good God
would not become a human being, nor would he be
bodily present under the form of ordinary bread and
wine. Francis repeatedly insisted on the fact that the
Eucharist was truly the Body and Blood of the Lord.
In fact he uses the phrase 'Body and Blood of the Lord'
numerous times throughout his Writings.

It is both interesting and fascinating that Francis re-enacted the Bethlehem scene of the Lord's birth within the celebration of the Eucharist at Greccio. We have already given a detailed account of this scene when we reflected on Francis's devotion to the Child Jesus. Now we can develop this further by showing how deeply Francis entered into the mystery of God with us, by linking the birth of the God-man with his Body and Blood in the Eucharist, made present for us every day when Mass is celebrated. To perceive this amazing truth requires faith and that, alas, was what Francis deemed lacking in so many ways. In *Admonition One*, Francis pleads for a faith-filled and converted heart regarding the Real Presence of Christ. 'Therefore, children, how long will you be hard of heart ... As he revealed Himself to the holy apostles in true flesh, so He reveals himself to us now in sacred bread.'[10]

Francis realised that one needs to exercise the gift of faith in order to embrace this sacred mystery. Therefore, he is very concerned with spiritual blindness, which prevents us from recognising the humanity and divinity of the Son of God in this Sacrament. To see with the eyes of faith requires a pure and converted heart, and he returns to this theme in several of his letters. This reflects the teaching of the Fourth Lateran Council, which stressed the need to repent of sin and receive Holy Communion at least once a year. However, Francis did not receive the Body and Blood of the Lord as a matter of obligation. His was an intimate, ardent and loving response to the humble, totally self-giving and self-emptying love of God. 'Toward the Sacrament of the Lord's Body he burned with fervour to his very marrow, and with unbounded wonder of that loving condescension and condescending love. He received Communion frequently and so devoutly that he made others devout.'[11] In an age when frequent Communion was not the norm, it is significant that Francis differed in this respect.

Understanding the immensity of the mystery before him, Francis was meticulous regarding the way in which the Body and Blood of the Lord was reserved and carried. His *Letter to the Clerics* very clearly expresses his grave concerns. 'Consider how very dirty are the chalices, corporals and altar-linens upon which His Body and Blood are sacrificed. It is placed and left in many dirty places, carried about unbecomingly, received unworthily, and administered to others without discernment'. We know that Francis cleaned the churches, and enlisted the help of St Clare and her sisters in the monastery of San Damiano to provide new homespun corporals and altar linens for almost all the churches in and around Assisi. 'The soft cloth made by Lady Clare's spinning she used to make many corporals and the cases to hold them, covered with silk or precious cloth'.[12] These linens were blessed by the Bishop of Assisi and given to the friars who took them personally to the various churches. In addition to the altar linens, Francis wanted the chalices and ciboria to be made of precious materials. Such was the profound love, care, respect, dignity and honour with which the Franciscan family held the Body and Blood of the Lord that Pope John Paul II presented St Francis as an example for today, saying: 'St Francis set down for his friars that the chalices, vessels and linens for the Eucharist have a particular dignity and should be treated with the highest respect and veneration'.[13]

Francis's ardent love and living faith enabled him to see with the eyes of his heart the wondrous mystery of the Eucharist and he realised that there would be no Eucharist without the priest. He was not unaware of the state of the priesthood and the religious laxity of some priests, yet with the eyes of faith he saw a deeper reality: 'We must revere the clergy not so much for themselves, if they are sinners, but because of their office and administration of the most holy Body and Blood of Christ which they sacrifice on the altar, receive and administer to others.'[14] For this reason, Francis always held priests in high esteem, so much so that he states in his Testament.

> The Lord gave me, and gives me still, such faith in priests who live according to the rite of the holy Roman Church because of their orders that, were they to persecute me, I would still want to have recourse to them.[15]

Celano remembered this when he wrote his biography of Francis. 'He wanted great reverence shown to the hands of priests, since they have the divinely granted authority to bring about this mystery'.[16] Francis linked the anointed hands of the priest, and the care of the altar vessels and linens, to the pure and precious body of the Virgin Mary who carried the Son of the eternal Father.

> Behold, each day He humbles Himself as when He came from the royal throne (Ws 18:15; Ph 2:8) into the Virgin's womb; each day He Himself comes to us, appearing humbly; each day He comes down from the bosom of the Father (Jn 1:18) upon the altar in the hands of a priest.[17]

Just as Mary became 'His Palace, His Tabernacle and His Dwelling',[18] so too the anointed hands of the priest holds the living God at the altar. In his Encyclical on the Eucharist, Pope John Paul II describes Mary as 'the first tabernacle in history',[19] a woman of the Eucharist in her whole life. When the Pope speaks of the continuity of the birth of Jesus with the Eucharist, he extends the privilege of being a Christ bearer, to every person who received the Body and Blood of the Lord.

Before reflecting on the Cross and the Eucharist in the Writings of Francis, we will look at Thérèse's understanding of the continuity of the birth of Jesus and the Eucharist.

Thérèse: Bethlehem and The Eucharist

Like Francis eight centuries before her, Thérèse had a profound love and an intense longing for Holy Communion. We can find many parallels in Francis's and Thérèse's attitudes, approach to, and understanding of the Real Presence of Christ in this Sacrament. We can also see parallels in the historical context in which they find themselves, living as they did in times of reform, renewal and a revival of Eucharistic devotion.

Unlike Francis, Thérèse was not actually involved in reform within the Church; rather she was caught up in the renewal and revival that were characteristic of her era. Nevertheless we see signs in her of a reformed attitude towards the Eucharist, especially frequent reception of Holy Communion, which was not customary at that time. This is demonstrated in the following words of Thérèse: 'Jesus gave Himself to me in Holy Communion more frequently than I would have dared hope. I'd take as a rule of conduct to receive, without missing a single one, the Communions my confessor permitted, allowing him to regulate the number and not asking'[20]. What Thérèse was probably referring to here was the Church's legislation at that time regarding frequent reception of the Eucharist. According to the decree of Pope Leo XIII a confessor could give permission for more frequent Communion but he had exclusive powers in this regard. Later, Thérèse sought permission from her Confessor to receive our Lord in Holy Communion on a frequent basis, that is on all the principal Feasts. In fact her sister, Celine, tells of a prophecy of Thérèse regarding daily Communion. Thérèse predicted that it would not be long after her death when every sister in the Lisieux Carmel would enjoy the privilege of daily Communion. Celine testified that this prophecy was fulfilled to the letter in the following way. The chaplain to the Lisieux Carmel, Father Youf, died a few days after Thérèse. His successor, Father Hodierne, empowered by Pope Leo's Decree, immediately introduced the practice of daily Communion for the sisters.

While we do not have any details of Francis's First Holy Communion, that of Thérèse is well documented by herself. 'The time of my First Communion remains engraved in my heart as a memory without any clouds. Jesus wished to make me taste a joy as perfect as is possible in this vale of tears'.[21] She tells us that this meeting with Jesus in Holy Communion was not just a meeting of friends but it was a fusion of hearts. What an amazing grace for an eleven-year-old child! She described this day as 'the beautiful day of days'. Although Thérèse was reluctant to try to express in human language her experience of that day, she did say it was the first kiss of Jesus and it was the kiss of love. Obviously she was absorbed in God in a way that cannot be fully expressed in words and she was filled with a deep longing to receive Jesus again. As already mentioned, frequent Communion was not the norm but Thérèse, having grown in confidence in Carmel did ask her confessor for permission to receive Holy Communion more frequently. She says:

> At this time in my life, I didn't have the boldness I now have, for I'm very sure a soul must tell her confessor the attraction she feels to receive her God. It is not to remain in a golden ciborium that he comes to us each day from heaven; it's to find another heaven, infinitely more dear to Him than the first: the heaven of our soul, made to His image, the living temple of the adorable Trinity.[22]

This permission was granted and it shows that Thérèse had an extraordinary awareness of the Real Presence of Jesus in this Sacrament.

Thérèse was brought up in a very pious home where devotion to the Eucharist was central. Her parents attended morning Mass on a daily basis, and visits to the Blessed Sacrament were part of her daily walks with her father. These visits happened even before her First Holy Communion so her devotion was being nurtured during these precious visits, where she thought of Jesus as a prisoner of love. A kiss of love, a prisoner of love—already love is the central experience, one that will come to full fruition as her spiritual journey develops.

What we find in Thérèse, which is very similar to Francis, is an appreciation of the humble, hidden presence of the Almighty and Eternal God in the small and very ordinary form of bread, in continuity with the mystery of the Incarnation. It is particularly in her poetry that Thérèse expounds this particular aspect of the Lord's self-giving and she does so in the context of the humble birth in Bethlehem, emphasising the role of Mary, Virgin and Mother. Her first poem, 'The Divine Dew', the name she gives to the virginal milk of Mary, Thérèse links the infancy of Jesus with His presence in the Eucharist. In Verse Five she says, 'This Dew hides in the sanctuary … Yes, behold, this Word made Host'.[23]

Like Francis, the Eucharist was for Thérèse her daily bread, her food and her nourishment. 'Living Bread, Bread of Heaven, divine Eucharist, O sacred Mystery! That love has brought forth … Come live in my heart, Jesus, my white Host, Just for today'.[24] Thérèse realised that Holy Communion is a food that in our poverty we need on a daily basis. When a novice was reluctant to receive Communion because of feelings of unworthiness, Thérèse reassured her that the Bread of Angels comes to strengthen and supply what is wanting. Towards the end of her life, very much aware of her own weakness and poverty, Thérèse again referred to the life-giving Bread of Life.

> You remain still in this valley of tears, hidden beneath the appearances of a white Host. Eternal Eagle, You desire to nourish me with Your divine substance and yet I am but a poor little thing who would return to nothingness if Your divine glance did not give me life from one moment to the next.[25]

Like Francis, Thérèse knew it was through the eyes of faith that she encountered the person of Jesus in the Eucharist: 'Living Bread of faith, Celestial Food, O mystery of love! My daily Bread, Jesus, is You'.[26]

Reminiscent of Francis creating the live crib at Greccio at the time of Midnight Mass, what Francis acted out visually Thérèse presented through verse.

She made connections with the Incarnation and the Eucharist and this is especially evident in her poem 'My Desires Near Jesus Hidden in His Prison of Love'.[27] In this poem, she speaks of the tabernacle key, which she envies because 'Each day you can open the prison of the Eucharist where the God of love resides'. In another verse she likens the Altar Stone to the blessed stable where Jesus was born, realising like Francis, that in every Mass He is born again on the Altar in the hands of the priest. The Corporal where Jesus rests she compares to the humble swaddling clothes in which Mary wrapped Him. She then turns to Mary and asks her to change her heart into a pure, beautiful Corporal to receive the white Host.

Like Francis, Thérèse was very attentive to the sacred vessels and altar linens. She loved being Sacristan, and her sister, Celine, said she fulfilled this duty with loving eagerness because of her ardent love for Jesus in the Blessed Sacrament. Thérèse also composed a poem entitled 'The Sacristans of Carmel'[28] in which she outlines the sweet office that prepares everything that is necessary to bring Heaven to earth every morning. Therese is in awe of this wonderful mystery and it leads her to consider 'the sublime mission of the Priest'. As Donald Kinney points out in his commentary on this poem, Thérèse realises that her burning desire to be a priest cannot be fulfilled. However, in this poem she finds her own concrete way of sharing in the 'sublime mission of the priest'. How does she do this? Transformed into Jesus by the Eucharist, changed into Him, she too, like the priest becomes 'another Christ'.[29] Therefore, transformation into Christ is the key. We know that Thérèse fervently prayed after each Communion, 'I live now, not I, but

Christ lives in me'. This realisation of transformation in and through the Eucharist dawned on Thérèse long before even her first reception of Holy Communion. One evening listening to Pauline's preparation of Celine, her older sister, for her First Communion, Thérèse writes, 'I heard you say that from the time one received one's First Communion, one had to commence living a new life, and I immediately made the resolution not to wait for that day but to commence the very same time as Celine'.[30] This is a remarkable observation for a little girl and still more remarkable that she put it into practice. In other words, through the Eucharist she brought life to the Gospel and the Gospel to life. In his General Audience on 6 April 2011, Pope Benedict captured this truth beautifully: 'Inseparable from the Gospel, for Thérèse the Eucharist was the Sacrament of Divine Love that stoops to the extreme to raise us to him'.

Thérèse was very much aware of the human weaknesses she saw in particular priests, yet like Francis, with a deep spirit of faith she saw beyond their faults, and respected them for their priesthood through which they make Christ present for us. Thérèse did all in her power to support priests by her prayer and life of sacrifice in Carmel.

We know that in 1895 the prioress, her sister Pauline (Mother Agnes of Jesus), told Thérèse that she had received a letter from a young seminarian who wished to have a sister in Carmel who would pray for him and offer sacrifices for him as he set out with missionary zeal to save souls. Thérèse was overjoyed that she was chosen to be a sister to this seminarian, Maurice Belliere, whom she would look upon as a brother thus associating herself with the priesthood in a most intimate way. Not long after this, Thérèse was asked to accept another seminarian as a brother, Adolphe Roulland, and to help him with her prayer and sacrifices. He was ordained in 1896 and became a missionary in China. Maurice Belliere was not ordained until after Thérèse's death. In and through her prayerful and sacrificial involvement with the ministry of these two priests in particular, Thérèse was deeply associated with the missionary work of the Church. To her great delight, she in turn was promised a daily remembrance at the altar when her brother-priests celebrated Mass.

PREPARING TO BRING HEAVEN TO EARTH

Both Francis and Thérèse understood the continuity of the birth of Christ with the Eucharist, not only as a banquet, feeding and nourishing the person as Bread of Life, of also as the redemptive sacrifice of the Body and Blood of Christ. Therefore they deeply understood that 'The most holy Eucharist contains the Church's entire spiritual wealth: Christ Himself, our passover and living bread'.[31]

Francis: Calvary and The Eucharist

In concentrating on the humanity of Christ, especially the Babe of Bethlehem and the suffering Christ of Calvary, Francis addressed two of the main religious reasons for the decline in Eucharistic practice in the thirteenth century. According to the Franciscan scholar, Norbert Nguyen-Van-Khanh, in Francis's time the humanity of Christ was neglected and ordinary people saw the Eucharist as an awesome mystery, to be approached with fear and dread. 'In their one-sided view of Christ as the all-powerful God, Lord, and supreme Judge of the universe, they forgot that Christ was also a human being, our brother, and our advocate with the Father'.[32] The second reason followed logically from the first. As the faithful experienced a God Who was to be feared, they felt very distant from Him and did not consider themselves to be worthy to receive Him. Consequently there was a separation of sacrifice from sacrament. The faithful would assist at Mass but would not receive Holy Communion. This problem was not new but it reached crisis point during Francis's lifetime.

Faithful to the concerns of the Fourth Lateran Council, Francis did not make distinctions that led to abuse or neglect of either the sacrificial or sacramental aspects of the Eucharist. Instead, as we have already noted, he speaks of the Eucharist within the total mystery of God's extravagant love, linking birth, death and resurrection. 'His Father's will was such that His blessed and glorious Son, Whom He gave to us and Who was born for us, should offer Himself through His own blood as a sacrifice and oblation on the altar of the Cross'.[33] Francis was well aware of the reality of the Mass as a redemptive sacrifice, the means of salvation for all people of all time, and he spoke of it many times in his writings. When he sent greetings to the General Chapter of the brothers, he did so in the context of the redemptive sacrifice of Christ's Body and Blood saying, 'Brother Francis, a worthless and weak man, your very little servant sends his greetings in Him Who has redeemed and washed us in His most precious Blood'.[34] Later in this same address Francis reminded his brothers who were priests that 'whenever they wish to celebrate Mass, being pure, they offer the true Sacrifice of the most holy Body and Blood of our Lord Jesus Christ'.[35]

The love of Francis for the Person of Christ as both humble baby and Suffering Servant led him to recognise the depth of self-giving in God that loves unto the end, even to death on the Cross. This is especially evident when Francis, (possibly influenced by 1P 2:24–25) writes about Jesus as our Shepherd and Guardian who both feeds us and lays down His life for us: 'Let us have recourse to Him, as to the Shepherd and Guardian of our souls, Who says, "I am the Good Shepherd, I feed my sheep and I lay down my life for My sheep"'.[36] It is easy to see that for Francis the Paschal Mystery, which will continue to the end of time, is the fulfilment of the

Incarnation. Always practical, Francis constantly encourages and admonishes his followers to follow in the footsteps of Christ, and he chooses the image of The Good Shepherd to clarify what Eucharistic living really means when Christ is taken literally. Francis ardently desired to follow the example of Christ in total self-giving through poverty, humility and love.

> Let all of us, brothers, consider the Good Shepherd Who bore the suffering of the cross to save His sheep. The Lord's sheep followed Him in tribulation and persecution, in shame and hunger, in weakness and temptation, and in other ways; and for these things they received eternal life from the Lord. Therefore, it is a great pity for us, the servants of God, that the saints have accomplished great things and we want only to receive glory and honour by recounting them.[37]

Faithful to the Gospel, Francis lived what he taught and he was especially aware that the most powerful teaching is through personal example more than words. For him, loving like Jesus meant laying down his life for others. Therefore, the new Covenant, the New Commandment to love, given before Jesus endured his passion and death, was all-important. Though he was not a priest, Francis's depth of understanding of the Eucharist as sacrifice and sacrament, as a bond of unity in love, led him to imitate his Lord with a deeply symbolic gesture with Eucharistic overtones. Francis, when he was dying, asked his distressed brothers to bring him some loaves of bread. He was too ill to break the bread himself but he asked the brothers to do this for him and then he gave a piece to each one to eat.

> Just as the Lord desired to eat with His apostles on the Thursday before His death, it seemed to those brothers that, in a similar way, blessed Francis, before his death, wanted to bless them and, in them, all the other brothers, and that they should eat that blessed bread as if in some way they were eating with the rest of their brothers.[38]

This sign of mutual love and union with one another in and through and with Christ in the Eucharist is a timeless truth that was beautifully expressed in the first century by St Paul in his First Letter to the Corinthians.

> The blessing-cup which we bless, is it not a sharing in the body of Christ; and the loaf of bread that we break, is it not a sharing in the body of Christ? And as there is one loaf, so we, although there are many of us, are one single body, for we all share in the one loaf (1 Co 10:16–17).

In the twenty-first century this same truth was reaffirmed by Blessed Pope John Paul II when he referred to the unifying power of the Eucharist, quoting St John Chrysostom's profound and perceptive commentary on St Paul's words: 'For what is the bread? It is the body of Christ. And what do those who receive it become? The Body of Christ—not many bodies but one body.'[39] How well Francis understood and lived this mystery.

Thérèse: Calvary and The Eucharist

Thérèse was very conscious of the Eucharist as a sacred banquet and daily nourishment for the soul, yet like Francis, she did not neglect the Eucharist as a sacrifice of the Body and Blood of the Lord. Perhaps even more so than Francis, she concentrated on the sacrificial aspect of the Eucharist, but always in the context of love, a consequence perhaps of her understanding of her Carmelite vocation.

In her Act of Oblation, Thérèse offered herself as a victim sacrifice, united with Christ on the Cross. She realised that in offering herself in union with Jesus her Spouse and Saviour 'the infinite treasures of His merits are mine'.[40] In her own inimitable way, her poetry reveals her awareness of the connection between Calvary and the Eucharist, referring to the Altar as 'the new Calvary where his Blood still flows for me'.[41] Thérèse was deeply aware of the timelessness of the Eucharistic sacrifice, an unchanging truth which Blessed John Paul II again brings to our attention. 'This sacrifice is so decisive for the salvation of the human race that Jesus Christ offered it and returned to the Father only after he had left us a means of sharing in it as if we had been present there'.[42]

Thérèse also understood and lived the truth expounded by the Second Vatican Council in the Dogmatic Constitution of the Church, *Lumen Gentium* 11, which is reflected in her Act of Oblation: 'Taking part in the Eucharistic Sacrifice, which is the source and summit of the whole Christian life, the faithful offer the divine victim to God, and offer themselves along with it'. This is what Thérèse did. She offered herself as a victim of love as Christ did on the Cross, and the inspiration to do so came while she was at Mass on Trinity Sunday 9 June 1895.

After prayer and reflection, Thérèse asked permission of her Prioress, Mother Agnes of Jesus, to offer herself as a victim of love in a personal Act of Oblation, which she would compose. Two days later, on 11 June, Thérèse knelt before the shrine of the miraculous Virgin of the Smile, who had cured her in her childhood, and recited her prayer of self-offering. Thérèse always emphasised that her offering was not as a victim of Divine Justice, which presupposes taking upon oneself the punishment reserved to sinners. Many Carmelites in Thérèse's lifetime did this, but Thérèse said that, great though such an offering might be, it did not appeal to her. Instead, she wanted to offer herself to love and receive from God all the love, the merciful love, He desires to pour out on his creatures, many of whom do not know it, or knowing it ignore or reject it. In acting like this, Thérèse united herself to Jesus, Who offered Himself in loving and total surrender to the will of the Father on behalf of us all. 'No one can have greater love than to lay down his life for his friends' (Jn 15:13). Thérèse had always ardently desired to lay down her life for the salvation of souls and her Act of Oblation gave her life a sacrificial dimension. Like Mary, the Mother of God who 'made her own the sacrificial dimension of the Eucharist'. In her daily preparation for Calvary, Mary experienced a kind of 'anticipated Eucharist'—one might say a 'spiritual communion'—of desire and of oblation, which would culminate with her union with her Son in his passion.[43] Thérèse also wanted the Eucharist to remain always in her as in a tabernacle and prayed to Jesus saying, 'Are You not all-powerful? Stay in me as You do in the tabernacle, and never leave this little host of Yours'.[44]

Prior to her Act of Self-Oblation, Thérèse had already written about the transforming power of the Eucharist. In one of her poems she expresses her joy at being chosen 'among the grains of pure Wheat who lose their lives for Jesus', and she begs the Lord to transform her into Himself. In this same poem she calls on Mary, asking her to 'change my heart'.[45] This childlike trust in Mary enabled Thérèse to enter into the mystery of the transforming power of the Eucharist, which her Act of Oblation explains and expands. Thérèse lived a Eucharistic life in the sense that like Christ, her life in all its mundane detail was blessed, broken and given with a totality that was extraordinary in its excess of love and abandonment to the will and good pleasure of God.

Francis and Thérèse: Saints of the Eucharist

It would seem that throughout the ages, the Church reaffirms certain truths and doctrines with a timely significance and relevance. This often happens when some aspect or dimension is over-exaggerated or perhaps ignored altogether. We have seen that Francis and Thérèse had a profound love for and understanding of the mystery of the Eucharist. They understood that 'The Mass is at the same time, and inseparably, the sacrificial memorial in which the sacrifice of the Cross is perpetuated and the sacred banquet of communion with the Lord's Body and Blood.'[46] They also had a graced insight into the continuity of the Incarnation in the mystery of the Eucharist and Its significance in our lives, a reality beautifully expressed by Pope John Paul II.

> The Eucharist, while commemorating the passion and resurrection, is also in continuity with the Incarnation. At the Annunciation Mary conceived the Son of God in the physical reality

of His Body and Blood, thus anticipating within herself what to some degree happens sacramentally in every believer who receives under the signs of bread and wine, the Lord's Body and Blood.[47]

From our two Saints we can discover anew the wonderful gift of the Eucharist in our lives and the consequences for our personal becoming and transformation in daily living and relationships. In this discovery we will also usher in the Kingdom of God, in union with Mary, whom Francis and Thérèse never fail to place before our eyes as Mother and example. Saints of the Eucharist in every era continue to give Mary a central role in the knowledge that she was the first dwelling place for the Son of God on this earth.

> Gazing upon Mary, we come to know *the transforming power present in the Eucharist.* In her we see the world renewed in love. Contemplating her, assumed body and soul into heaven, we see opening up before us those 'new heavens' and that 'new earth' which will appear at the second coming of Christ. Here below, the Eucharist represents their pledge, and in a certain way, their anticipation: *'Veni, Domine Jesu!'* (Rev 22:20).[48]

Reflection

How is your life being transformed by the Eucharist as it is blessed, broken and given for others?

Notes

1   R. J. Armstrong, OFMCap., W. J. A. Hellmann, OFMConv., W. J. Short, OFM., *Francis of Assisi The Saint Early Documents,* vol. I, (London, New York: New City Press, 2000), p. 118.

2   A. Bancroft, *St Thérèse of Lisieux Poems,* (London: Harper-Collins, 1996), p. 51.

3   Pope John Paul II, *Ecclesia de Eucharistia,* 62.

4   *Ibid.,* 11.

5   For fuller explanations see *Pope John Paul II Directory on Popular Piety and The Liturgy, Principles and Guidelines,* and N. Nguyen-Van-Khahn, OFM., *The Teacher of His Heart. Jesus Christ in the Thoughts and Writings of St Francis,* (New York: The Franciscan Institute, Franciscan Pathways, 1994), p. 153.

6   R. J. Armstrong, OFMCap., W. J. A. Hellmann, OFMConv., W. J. Short, OFM., *Francis of Assisi The Founder Early Documents,* vol. II, (London, New York: New City Press, 2000), p. 214.

7   Armstrong et al., *Francis of Assisi The Saint,* vol. I, p. 118.

8   *Ibid.,* p. 159.

9   *Ibid.,* p. 129.

10 *Ibid.,* p. 129.

11 Armstrong *et al., Francis of Assisi The Founder,* vol. II, p. 375.

12 R. J. Armstrong, OFM., (Edited and Translated) *Clare of Assisi Early Documents,* (New York: Paulist Press, 1988), p. 152.

13 Synod of Bishops XI, *Lineamenta,* 50.

14 Armstrong *et al., Francis of Assisi The Saint,* vol. I, p. 47.

15 *Ibid.,* p. 125.

16 Armstrong *et al., Francis of Assisi The Founder,* vol. II, p. 376.

17 Armstrong *et al., Francis of Assisi The Saint,* vol. I, p. 129.

18 *Ibid.,* p. 163

19 Pope John Paul II, *Ecclesia de Eucharistia,* 53, 55.

20 J. Clarke, OCD., *Story of a Soul, The Autobiography of St Thérèse of Lisieux,* (Washington DC: ICS Publications, 1972), p. 104.

21 *Ibid.,* p. 73.

22 *Ibid.,* p. 104.

23 D. Kinney, ODC., (Trans) *The Poetry of Saint Thérèse of Lisieux,* (Washington DC: ICS Publication, 1995), p. 38.

24 *Ibid.*, p. 52.
25 Clarke, *Story of a Soul,* p. 199.
26 Kinney, *The Poetry of Saint Thérèse of Lisieux*, p. 130.
27 *Ibid.*, pp. 133–5.
28 *Ibid.*, p. 169
29 *Ibid.*, pp. 169–170.
30 Clarke, *Story of a Soul,* p. 57.
31 Pope John Paul II, *Ecclesia de Eucharistia,* 1.
32 N. Nguyen-Van-Khanh, OFM., *The Teacher of His Heart Jesus Christ in the Thought and Writings of St Francis,* (New York: The Franciscan Institute, Franciscan Pathways, 1994), p. 156.
33 Armstrong *et al., Francis of Assisi The Saint,* vol. I, p. 46.
34 *Ibid.*, p. 116.
35 *Ibid.*, p. 117.
36 *Ibid.*, p. 80.
37 *Ibid.*, p. 131.
38 Armstrong *et al., Francis of Assisi The Founder,* vol. II, p. 135.
39 Pope John Paul II, *Ecclesia de Eucharistia,* 23.
40 Clarke, *Story of a Soul,* p. 276.
41 Kinney, *The Poetry of Saint Thérèse of Lisieux*, p. 134.
42 Pope John Paul II, *Ecclesia de Eucharistia,* 11.
43 *Ibid.*, 56.
44 C. O' Mahony, *St Thérèse of Lisieux by those who knew her, Testimonies from the Process of Beatification,* (Dublin: Veritas, 1975), p. 237.
45 Kinney, *The Poetry of Saint Thérèse of Lisieux*, pp. 134–5.
46 Pope John Paul II, *Ecclesia de Eucharistia,* 12.
47 *Ibid.*, 55.
48 *Ibid.*, 62.

Chapter 6

The Primacy of Love

*The love of Him who loved us greatly is greatly
to be loved.*[1]

St Francis

*Jesus! I would so love Him! Love Him as never
yet He has been loved.*[2]

St Thérèse

I n previous chapters we have looked at the spirituality of Francis and Thérèse giving particular
attention to the centrality of the Word of God in the
light of the Crib, the Cross and the Eucharist. We now
focus on love, which permeates and underpins every
aspect of their lives and the message and mission that
is their legacy. Francis and Thérèse simply re-pre-
sented the Good News of the Gospel, whose central
message is the revelation of God Whose essence and
being is Love. Centuries before, St John had stated it
very simply and directly: 'God is love' (1Jn 4:8) and he
emphasised that it is not our love for God but God's
love for us that is the revelation. Sometimes this central
message of God's love may be clouded, deformed or
neglected altogether by cult, sect, heresy or other forms
of imbalanced teaching. Thankfully there are men and
women in every age who call us back to the heart of
the Gospel message, the Good News of God's extravagant love. Francis and Thérèse are among this number.

Love originates in the Trinity, the inexhaustible
source and reality, enveloped in mystery yet embodied
in the Person of Jesus Christ. To enter more deeply into
this mystery of love at the heart of the Trinity and the
way in which we are caught up in it, we will explore
with Francis and Thérèse their relationships with the
Trinity, with their brothers and sisters, with the whole
of creation, and the invitation and challenge they hold
out to us.

St Francis and the Father's Love

Francis never wrote an autobiography, yet his deepest
feelings and thoughts are revealed in his Writings, and
his biographers have captured the essence of his life,

his message and his mission. From both sources, Francis emerges as a man on fire with the love of God, and he discovered this Divine Fire first and foremost in the heart of the Trinity, lavishly poured into every heart open to receive it.

Journeying into the heart of God was a life-long experience for Francis. At the very beginning of his journey he was so overjoyed by his newly found love that his friends thought he was in love with a young lady and teased him about getting married. Francis replied that he would take a bride more beautiful than they had ever seen, one who surpassed all others in beauty and wisdom. Of course they did not understand—at least not until very much later. The important point is that it was love that lured the heart of Francis, and only spousal, mystical language could express his experience at this moment in his young life. This was just the beginning and, like all beginnings, they hold the promise and potential of what is to come. The spousal attraction and promise at the beginning, matured into the intimacy of total union and identification on Mount La Verna. So how did the journey into love evolve for Francis?

From what we have said already about the Crib, the Cross and the Eucharist, it is obvious that Francis fell in love with a God who humbled Himself to meet us in our littleness and poverty. This God whom Francis addressed as 'All-powerful, most holy, Almighty and supreme God ... Without beginning and end, unchanging, invisible, indescribable, ineffable ...' is also the 'Most Holy Father ... gentle, lovable delightful and desirable' and the giver of all good gifts, especially His most beloved Son, Jesus, and the Holy Spirit the Paraclete.[3] The Father is the source of all goodness and love, and with great insight and sensitivity Francis recognised the self-giving and self-emptying love of the Father in giving us His Son. Little wonder then that Francis received the Son with all his heart and soul and desired to become like him in every way possible. Jesus, the image of the invisible God, was for Francis not only the human face of God but also the One Who reflected his own face back to him and became his way back to the Father.

Immersed in the mystery of love, Francis learned from Jesus, who is nearest the Father's heart, the meaning and depth of the extravagant love in the Father's heart and gradually entered the depths of its mystery. The Father, who is the source of all that is: the creation, the incarnation, the redemption, the resurrection—everything is His initiative. Francis is overwhelmed by such excessive and gratuitous love, exclaiming: 'We thank You for Yourself, for through Your holy will and through Your only Son with the Holy Spirit, You have created everything.' Still addressing the Father, Francis reflects on the love with which the Father gave His own Son: 'Through Your holy love with which You loved us You brought about His birth ... and You willed to redeem us through His Cross.' Then Francis prays: 'We humbly ask our Lord Jesus Christ, Your beloved Son, in Whom You were well pleased, together with the Holy Spirit, the Paraclete, to give You thanks, for everything.'[4] Later he would compose his *Canticle of Creation* in an outburst of praise and thanksgiving. Steeped in the Father's love, Francis realised that it is Jesus who reveals the humble, selfless, excessive love within the Father's heart and it is through Him, with Him and in Him that he will return love for love.

Francis opened his heart to the revelation of the Father's love when he first gazed upon the Crucifix in the little Church of San Damiano. Though still at the beginning of his journey, we can glimpse something of this mystical encounter more by what Francis does not say than by what he actually says. Like all mystical encounters, it is difficult to clothe the experience in human words even to oneself, and this is exactly what happened to Francis. 'He felt this mysterious change in himself, but he could not describe it',[5] but we are told that from that moment on, compassion for Christ crucified was deeply imprinted within his heart. The love of the Father in giving His Son to free us from suffering by taking it upon Himself, even to dying upon the Cross is the ultimate in love's compassionate expression. Francis, who desired to follow in the footsteps of Jesus, must also embrace and reflect the same loving compassion that Jesus embodied. This he did first and foremost in his embrace of the leper and his subsequent service to his brother lepers, but also in the way in which he expressed fraternal love and compassion for all his brothers and sisters, including the whole of creation.

It is very interesting that Francis had such a special relationship with God as Father, especially in the light of his very strained relationship with his own father. His biographers describe that dramatic event at the beginning of his conversion when Francis declared before the Bishop and people of Assisi, his hometown: 'From now on I will say freely: "Our Father, who art in heaven", and not "My father, Pietro de Bernardone".'[6] These may seem like harsh words, but Francis had suffered much at the hands of his father who did not understand his vocation to renounce everything and follow Christ in poverty and humility. Yet, in the plan of God, Who works everything to a person's good when they trust Him completely, this gesture of Francis would lead him to a privileged experience of the Fatherhood of God, through the experience of union with Jesus, the most beloved Son of the Father, whether in sorrow or in joy.

When Francis was dying, he identified with Jesus, the beloved Son when he asked for the Gospel of John to be read. In the chosen passage set in the context of the Last Supper Discourses (Jn 14–17), Jesus, about to leave those who were most dear to Him, shared with them what was in His heart. Francis, about to leave this world and those who were closest to him, identified with Jesus when he prayed to the Father in the same personal and intimate way: 'Holy Father, keep those You have given me true to Your name, so that they may be one like us' (Jn 17:11). Like Jesus, this was the prayer of Francis for all his followers: to follow closely in the footsteps of the One who is the Way the Truth and the Life. Therefore, with awe and gratitude, humility and praise, Francis opened his heart to the Father's invitation to share in the sonship of Jesus, exclaiming: 'O how glorious it is to have a holy and great Father in Heaven!.'[7]

In his *Praises of God*,[8] written by Francis after receiving the stigmata, perhaps we have his most eloquent expression of the greatness of the Father. Franciscan scholar, Thaddee Matura, has pointed out that there is an element of surprise here because, 'After the Stigmata—a Christological event if ever there was one—we would expect a prayer or praise to Christ.' He goes on to point out that it is rather 'A pure admiring look, contemplation, whose object is the Trinitarian God, but whose centre is indicated by the words "holy Father". It is then a hymn to the Father as the principle of the Trinitarian mystery.'[9] Francis realised that the Father is the source of all that is most wonderful, especially the wonder of the Incarnation, God's presence among us in human flesh. Therefore, the love of the Father is most exquisitely expressed in His humility and extravagant love, identifying with us in our frailty in the gift of Jesus, the Word made flesh.

Francis and Jesus the Beloved Son

In his determined decision to follow as closely as possible in the footsteps of Jesus, the beloved Son of the Father, Francis entered into the very depths of the divine mystery of the Trinity, a communion of love and loving relationships. For him, Jesus was above all the Revealer of Trinitarian life and love. Therefore, Francis had one over-riding desire in this life: to walk in the footsteps of our Lord Jesus Christ and become like Him. This he did with such fidelity, intensity and originality that he has been called the most Christlike of men. 'The unconquerable enkindling of love in him for the good Jesus had grown into lamps and flames of fire that many waters could not quench so powerful a love.'[10]

Francis and Thérèse, and each one of us relate to Christ in ways that are particular and personal. Sometimes one dimension of relationship dominates and sometimes another. We know that in his following of Christ, Francis was deeply touched and influenced by many different aspects of the revelation of God in Christ, namely: Christ as Word, Wisdom, Light, Shepherd, Master, Brother, Spouse, Servant, Lord, King, Saviour, Redeemer and Beloved Son. We have already mentioned a number of these relationships already and others we will explore in the next chapter but in all of them, it is Jesus who is the Way, the Truth and the Life.

In his *First Admonition* Francis highlights this essential truth that Jesus revealed to His disciples, that he is 'The Way, the Truth and the Life and that no one can come to the Father except through Me.'[11] This is the bedrock on which Francis builds his life. This is why his brothers remembered that Jesus was always on the lips and in the heart of Francis. Celano states it very clearly and beautifully, saying:

> The brothers who lived with him know,
> that daily, constantly, talk of Jesus
> was always on his lips,
> sweet and pleasant conversations about Him,
> kind words full of love.
> Out of the fullness of the heart his mouth spoke.
> So the spring of radiant love
> that filled his heart within gushed forth.
> He was always with Jesus:
> Jesus in his heart,
> Jesus in his mouth,
> Jesus in his ears,
> Jesus in his eyes,
> Jesus in his hands,
> He bore Jesus always in his whole body.[12]

In our present context of the primacy of love—and God is love—it is striking to see how the Writings of Francis reveal just how deeply he became a beloved son in the Son. This truth could not become a reality in the life of Francis without the gift and presence of the Holy Spirit, Who alone gives the power to see with the eyes of the heart what is invisible to the human eye. In his *First Admonition* Francis explains this with great simplicity and profound insight that it is only through the Holy Spirit that we can really know the Father and the Son. 'He cannot be seen except in the Spirit.'[13] It is this relationship between the Father and the Son that is central for Francis, and he never ceases to seek to enter more fully into this mystery in which he too is embraced.

In his *Office of the Passion*,[14] Francis identifies most tenderly with Jesus in his experience of being the Son of the loving Father. With great familiarity, Francis translates and compiles the Psalms in such a way that, from birth to death, a picture emerges of the earthly life of Jesus as Son, and with great poignancy he lets us hear the many human emotions that fill the heart of the Son as he speaks with the Father, whom He addresses so many times as 'My most holy Father.' In many of these instances the emotions are anguish, fear, distress and desolation, especially as Jesus faces his painful agony and death. These emotions are balanced by the joy and exultation of the Risen life of the eternal Son united in glory with the Father. Francis takes us into the reality of the pain of life and the promise of eternal glory. Joy and sorrow are inseparable, and later in his life Francis will understand this in greater depth in his mystical experience on Mount La Verna.

With great realism Francis recognised that it is in our day-to-day living that we need the daily bread of the Father's love and forgiveness in His Son Jesus Christ. Therefore, he prayed the Lord's Prayer and wrote his own commentary on it, inviting us to turn to the Father Who is 'Our Creator, Redeemer, Consoler and Saviour.' If we can call on God as our Father, then it follows that we are all brothers and sisters within the family of God and like the first-born Son, Jesus, we too are called to a life of love. Like Jesus, Francis emphasised love of God and love of neighbour as the greatest Commandment and he added his own words when emphasising the primacy and totality of the Commandment to love, which embraces the whole of creation.

With our whole soul,
our whole mind,
with our whole strength and fortitude
with our whole understanding
with all our powers,
with every effort,
every affection,
every feeling,
every desire and wish
let us love the Lord God.[15]

Love such as this is the direct result of the inner dynamic of the Spirit of Love, whose presence and Divine activity Francis desired above all things.

Francis and the Spirit of Love

In his beautiful prayer at the end of his *Letter to the Entire Order*,[16] Francis is keenly aware of a graced movement of inward cleansing, interior enlightenment and the Fire of the Holy Spirit that inflames the heart. These movements suggest traditionally accepted stages of prayer as we journey into the depths of God's love. However, it is obvious that Francis does not view these movements of the Spirit in a linear way because this process is part of the human condition at all stages of our transformation. Purification, illumination and union are intertwined and inter-related in our on-going and deepening relationship with the Father, the Son and the Holy Spirit.

Throughout this transforming process, the symbolism of Fire is prominent. St Bonaventure, in the prologue to *The Major Life of St Francis*, tells us that Francis was 'totally aflame with a Seraphic fire'.[17] The reference to the Seraph is a biblical one, in which we find the prophet Isaiah, in the presence of the All Holy God, purified and prepared for mission (Is 6:2–7). The name Seraphim means 'the burning ones'. Fire, heat, burning and light are images we often find in the writings about Francis and in the Prayers and Writings of Francis himself, relating to the intensity of the burning love of God. What we discover is mutuality in intensity and desire in the heart of the Lover-God, and the beloved-Francis, and indeed with each one of us if we are open to it. It was especially on Mount La Verna that Francis experienced and marvelled at the mystery of such exceeding love. It was then he fully understood by Divine inspiration that the transformation that was taking place within him was rooted and grounded in the enkindling and enflaming of love. As the vision of Christ under the appearance of the Seraph was disappearing, 'It left in his heart a marvellous fire, and imprinted in his flesh a likeness of signs no less marvellous.'[18]

Francis, like Thérèse, had an intense desire for martyrdom. What Francis understood on Mount La Verna was that his martyrdom was one of love—not physical martyrdom as he had previously contemplated, especially when he was willing to take the Word of the Lord to those peoples and areas when martyrdom was a real possibility. St Bonaventure clearly makes the connection between martyrdom and love saying that on Mount La Verna Francis understood that he was to be 'totally transformed into the likeness of Christ crucified, not by the martyrdom of his flesh, but by the enkindling of his soul'.[19]

To reach this stage of complete union with God is possible for every person. It is the same inner force that creates, recreates, invites, fashions and shapes the human person in the image and likeness in which we are all created. To engage in this journey of transformation we are called, like Francis and Thérèse, to be people of immense, even infinite desires. Celano tells us that at the very beginning of his life while still seeking worldly glory, Francis was a man, 'seething with desire' but the Lord visited him and 'exalted and enticed to its pinnacle' his desire for glory.[20] The beginning of this transformation of desire continued to deepen in Francis, so much so that eventually Francis could say and even insert in his Rule, 'Pay attention to what they (the brothers) must desire above all else: to have the Spirit of the Lord and Its holy activity.'[21]

The holy activity of the Spirit of the Lord within Francis led him to distinguish the subtle but very real difference there is between doing the will of God and pleasing Him. We find reference to this distinction in at least two of his Writings: In his *Rule* he tells the brothers, 'We have nothing else to do but to follow the will of the Lord and to please Him.'[22] He repeats this sentiment in his *Letter to the Entire Order*, and makes this point quite clearly when he asks for the grace 'To do for You alone what we know You want us to do and always to desire what pleases You.'[23] We all know that there is a difference between doing what we know someone wants us to do, and intentionally setting out to please that person. We know that God's will is to lead us to Himself in ways that have been revealed to us throughout the history of Salvation and especially in the life and teaching of Jesus. We find there an overall Plan and general framework within which we are invited to respond. But when we desire to *please* God, a new dimension in our relationship emerges that is personal and unique and which leaves room for our own loving, creative and Spirit-led response. Such was the vocation of Francis and Thérèse. Both assure us that the same invitation and challenge is open to us. Did not Francis say, 'I have done what was mine to do; may Christ teach you what is yours.'[24] Francis could say this with the knowledge and conviction that he remained open and faithful to his own personal vocation to return love for love in a way that only he could. Therefore, he encouraged the brothers, and he also encourages us, to discover our unique way to God.

In the context of personal call and vocation and the discernment and challenge this poses, we have the example of Francis and Brother Leo having a heart to heart talk as they walked along the road. It seems obvious that Brother Leo was asking Francis for advice and this was given in a very personal way with maternal love and concern:

> My son, I speak to you in this way — as a mother would … In whatever way it seems better to you to please the Lord God and to follow His footprint and poverty, do it with the blessing of the Lord God and my obedience.[25]

According to the Franciscan scholar, Regis Armstrong, the advice that Francis gives Brother Leo, has sometimes been described as 'The Magna Carta of Franciscan Freedom.'[26] However, Armstrong argues that this may not be the case because the advice is given within the context of following the Lord's footprint and poverty. In the next chapter we will return to the individual call within the general framework in which Francis and his followers *please* God, the poverty of being a minor, a little one before the Lord.

Thérèse and the Father's Love

Unlike Francis, Thérèse enjoyed a close and loving relationship with her father. She paints an idyllic picture of her home life, especially Sunday evenings. The family played games, after which Thérèse and Celine would sit on their father's knee and listen to his beautiful singing or inspired poems. Finally they said family night prayers together and each child, according to age, received her father's goodnight kiss. Being the youngest, Thérèse was last in line and enjoyed the special attention she received as her father's little Queen. 'The Queen naturally came last and the King took her by the two elbows to kiss her and she would cry out in a high-pitched voice: "Good night, Papa, good night and sleep well".' As Sundays drew to a close, Thérèse experienced sadness and a sense of exile, so much so that she longed for Heaven, that 'Never-ending Sunday of the Fatherland.'[27]

Thérèse was well aware that she had a special place in her father's heart. Especially since the death of her mother, Thérèse tells us that 'she was surrounded by the most delicate tenderness. Our father's very affectionate heart seemed to be enriched now with a truly maternal love!.'[28] Her father was indulgent with her, buying her little presents even when there was no special occasion to celebrate. But Louis Martin gave his daughter the most precious gift of all: his loving and attentive presence. Father and child spent quality time together. Thérèse went with her father on his walks, his fishing trips, and his visits to Churches and to the poor. Holidays and pilgrimages were also spent in his company and as a loving father he was attentive to her every need. She recognised that she was possessive of his singular love for her. In recalling her childhood memories, Thérèse says, 'I cannot say how much I loved Papa; everything in him caused me to admire him.'[29] She then goes on to reason that if he was the King of France which she felt would be an honour for the whole country, she was glad he was not, because then she would not have him all to herself. Truly Thérèse experienced her father as incomparable, one in whom she could pour out her heart with the greatest confidence. This experience of understanding, confident, trusting, tender, kind, indulgent and unconditional love from her father laid the foundation that would influence her for the rest of her life in her relationship with God as Father.

We have mentioned elsewhere the illness of Thérèse's father and the anguish this caused within the family. The absence of Louis Martin at Thérèse's Profession caused her to declare in words almost identical to those of Francis, but prompted by different circumstances: 'On the day of my wedding I was really an orphan, no longer having a father on this earth and being able to look to Heaven with confidence, saying in all truth: "Our Father who art in Heaven".'[30] Whatever the experience of an earthly father, whether positive or negative, led Francis and Thérèse to throw themselves into the arms of God as Father. Certainly in the case of Thérèse, we can see very positive influences as her unique way to God developed between Father and child. Even on a rare occasion when her father was tired and showed some annoyance because Thérèse still expected her 'magic shoes' to be filled at Christmas, Thérèse overcame her sensitivity and hurt and let her father see only her joy and excitement. This attitude will also be prominent in her relationship with God as Father. Thérèse did not want God to see her suffering (if that were possible), she wanted only to love Him and give Him pleasure, or as Francis would say, 'to love Him and please Him'. The sentiments are the same.

Thérèse admitted that when she had difficulty in praying she would simply pray the Our Father very slowly and her soul was nourished. A novice recalled that she saw Thérèse rapt in prayer whilst sewing, and she asked her what she was thinking about. With tears in her eyes, Thérèse confided that she had been meditating on The Our Father, remarking, 'It is so sweet to call the good God our Father.'[31] She had a profound realisation of the excessive love of the Father made present in Jesus, but she also knew that without the Spirit of Love we cannot 'give the name "Father" to our Father in Heaven'.[32]

Like Francis, Thérèse experienced the goodness and love of the Father always in relation to the Son and the Holy Spirit. When speaking of the wonder of the Incarnation and the birth of Christ, Thérèse does so in the context of 'That luminous night which sheds such light on the delights of the Trinity.'[33] Significantly, it was on the Feast of the Holy Trinity that Thérèse received the grace to offer herself as a victim to Merciful Love. Others had offered themselves as victims to Divine Justice but it was love that attracted Thérèse. Her Act of Oblation begins with the words: 'O My God! Most Blessed Trinity, I desire to Love You and make You loved.' Later in this same prayer she thanks the Father for loving her so much as to give her His only Son as her Saviour and Spouse. Thérèse, like Francis, realised that the Father gives everything, even His only Son and she begs the Father to look upon her 'only in the face of Jesus and in His heart burning with love'.[34] She intuitively understood the communion of love that is the Trinity. This is expressed clearly and beautifully in her poems: 'The Spirit of Love sets me aflame with his fire. In loving You I attract the Father.'[35] There is no doubt that she attracted the Father and her love for Jesus is beyond question. Her sister, Celine, testified that Thérèse loved God the Father with all the tender affection of a daughter. She constantly invoked the Spirit of Love too. But "her Jesus" as she liked to call Him, was everything to her. It is to her love for Jesus that we will now turn.

Thérèse and Jesus the Beloved Son

Thérèse sees Jesus held captive by our love. This conviction was probably nurtured by Thérèse's understanding of the works of St John of the Cross. We know that when her sister, Celine, came to Carmel she brought with her a Notebook in which she had written her chosen texts from Scripture and from St John of the Cross. Thérèse had access to these texts, one of which explained the power of love that holds God a prisoner, submissive to what we want! In explaining the way in which Jesus is held captive by love in the smallest of ways, Thérèse in her own inimitable way uses the image from the Song of Songs, 'You ravish my heart, my sister, my promised bride, you ravish my heart with a single one of your glances, with a single link of your necklace.' (Sg 4:9) Using this text as a basis for her own thoughts, she writes a letter to her sister, Leonie, assuring her that God is not to be feared, he who is 'content with a glance, a sigh of love … who allows Himself be enchained by a hair fluttering on our neck!'.[36] This is the language of love. This is the science of love for which Thérèse longed. Such love was mutual. Such captivity was mutual. Therefore, Thérèse joyfully refers to herself as a prisoner for Jesus, for whom she had scorned all other joys.

Thérèse realised that love alone gives meaning and purpose to life. Nothing else counts. Nothing else is of value, not even the greatest, most brilliant or most heroic deeds, unless they are done for love. Of course St Paul had said it long ago in his *Letter to the Corinthians* (1Co 13), and Thérèse was familiar with this Letter because there she would discover her vocation within the Church: to be love. Therefore with inner conviction and from her own experience, she tells Leonie that 'perfection is a matter of taking hold of Jesus by His Heart'.[37] This is exactly what Thérèse did. Nothing held her back from love. Her faults and failings, her defects of character or personality, her sins—even if she had sinned grievously, could not prevent her from taking hold of Jesus by His heart. 'Even though I had on my conscience all the sins that can be committed, I would go, my heart broken with sorrow, and throw myself into Jesus's arms.'[38] When speaking to Mother Agnes, Thérèse confided the depth of her understanding and insight into the way of love. 'How sweet is the way of love, dear Mother. True, one can fall or commit infidelities, but, knowing how to draw profit from everything, love quickly consumes everything.'[39]

For Thérèse, Jesus was a friend, a brother, a consoler, a saviour, a shepherd, a King, a fiancée, and a bridegroom. Her Jesus was her way to the fullness of life and love within the heart of the Trinity. She asked Jesus to draw her into the flames of His love and to unite her so closely to Him that he could live in her, saying, 'I dare to ask You "to love those whom You have given me with the love with which You loved me".'[40] In this way Thérèse carried out the command of Jesus to love as he had loved. This was most obvious in her relationships with her family and school friends and later with her sisters in Carmel. Those who lived with her testified to her amazing sisterly love, day in and day out, in all circumstances and for all her sisters, without exception. In fact we know that she went out of her way to be in the company of those who had the most difficult temperaments and personalities. Thérèse had learned from her own experience that what worked for her probably worked for others too. 'No word of reproach touched me as much as did one of your caresses. My nature was such that fear made me recoil; with love not only did I advance, I actually flew.'[41] However, we must not assume that Thérèse was soft and sentimental in her relationships. On the contrary, she understood the meaning of love in the sense of choosing the best for the other person. When writing to her prioress, she recalled that when she was Novice Mistress, Thérèse was not only firm but also at times she was actually severe when dealing with her novices. This was not easy for Thérèse, she admits, 'What cost me more than anything else was to observe the faults and slightest imperfections and to wage war to the death on these.'[42] This observation and correction of faults and failings and Thérèse's response to them must be seen within the realm of her responsibility as Novice Mistress. Outside of this responsibility, she often admonished her sisters in community to overlook the faults and failings of others and look for their virtues instead. She said that true charity actually bears with the defects we find in one another. This is the human situation where love can triumph because we cannot ever make a judgement about what goes on in the hearts of others.

We know that the loving, gentle, accepting presence of Thérèse worked wonders within her community and we might be tempted to think this was easy for her. It was not. She admitted to Celine that the efforts she had to make in this area cost her a lot. It appears that Celine was surprised by this admission because Thérèse always made community living and loving look effortless. To love as Jesus loves is not possible for us unless, like Thérèse, we ask Jesus to love others with His own love in and through us. She realised that the more she was united with Jesus the more she was capable of loving all her sisters. Later in life she admitted that her love for her sisters in community was imperfect until Jesus enlightened her about His new Commandment to love as he loved. It was then that Thérèse understood and she addressed Jesus, saying, 'You know very well that never would I be able to love my Sisters as You love them, unless You, O my Jesus, loved them in me.'[43] In a letter to her cousin, Marie Guerin, Thérèse wrote, 'There exists but one Being capable of comprehending love; it is Jesus.'[44] From Jesus, Thérèse drew her strength to love and longed intensely to be consumed by the Spirit of Love, the Gift Jesus promised to send and without Whom such love would not be possible.

Thérèse and the Holy Spirit of Love

The Holy Spirit, the Spirit of Love has always been associated with fire and flame and there is an abundance of references to this symbolism in the writings of Thérèse. Like Francis, Thérèse identified with the intensity of Seraphic love, saying, 'In this furnace of love, I shall be consumed, and like a Seraphim, Lord, I shall love you.'[45] The intensity of her desire and longing are more frequently expressed after she had offered herself to Love in her Act of Oblation. Sometimes her yearning is for purification, sometimes for illumination and more often for transformation that leads to intimate union. As we have already pointed out, the Church recognises these stages of prayer, not necessarily in a linear way but in a cyclic way that happens as prayer deepens and the relationship with God intensifies. Thérèse does not outline stages or levels of prayer, as did Teresa of Avila and John of the Cross, yet we see the process clearly at work in her.

If we look first at Thérèse's experience of purifying love, we see clearly that she longs for and is convinced that the fire of love will purify all her failings. 'If through weakness I sometimes fall, may Your Divine Glance cleanse my soul immediately, consuming all my imperfections like the fire that transforms everything into itself.'[46] Therefore, Thérèse had no fear of Purgatory because she believed the Divine Fire of Love purified her in an instant. So sure was she of this purifying Fire that she wanted others to have the same confident trust in God's merciful love. Writing to Fr Maurice Belliere, a missionary Priest, who was by nature rather fearful of God and His judgements, Thérèse said, 'When we cast our faults with entire filial confidence into the devouring fire of love, how would these not be consumed beyond return?'[47] She too had suffered from scruples at different times during her life; therefore she was in a very good position to enlighten others regarding the merciful love of God.

Depth of insight and understanding of the purifying Fire of Love was part of the gift of illumination within the heart of Thérèse. Often she uses symbolic language to convey her experiences and some of these we will also refer to in our next chapter. Fire and flame are particularly prominent in her writings. Both suggest light, and she uses light in different contexts to impart her teaching and express what is happening in her relationship with God. Thérèse refers to herself as a child of light in one of her poems entitled 'Jesus, my beloved, Remember', in which she asks forgiveness for not always serving her King as well as she might.[48] Still in the context of light, when reflecting on love, she speaks of those who are seduced by a false love which she describes as a false light, saying that such souls 'Fly like poor moths and burn their wings, and then return to the real and gentle light of Love that gives them new wings ... so that they can fly towards Jesus, the Divine Fire "which burns without consuming"'.[49] Thérèse points out that had she been exposed to such a misleading light perhaps she too would have burned her wings!

Thérèse also compared God to the Sun, the greatest Light of all and, with all her heart she desired to gaze upon the Divine Sun from Whose rays she never strayed too far. Even when the Light remained hidden, the work of love continued because Therese was convinced in faith that she was being consumed by an undying and everlasting love. This conviction was not uttered from a heart filled with consolation and the felt experience of the nearness of God. Writing to Sister Marie of the Trinity, Thérèse says, 'Without support yet with support, living without Light, in darkness, I am wholly being consumed by love.'[50]

One with the Invisible Light within her, Thérèse knows that God Himself has given us a means to lift us and the world to Himself and she uses two striking images to illustrate this: the lever and the elevator. Both images are grounded in love. Regarding the former, Thérèse included St Francis as one of those Saints who drew on this divine science in the context of which she quoted Archimedes, 'Give me a lever and a fulcrum and I lift the world.' Explaining further, Thérèse pointed out the advantage the Saints had over Archimedes. 'The almighty has given them as fulcrum: Himself Alone; as lever: prayer which burns with a fire of love.'[51] Using the image of the elevator, Thérèse was aware that this new invention in some homes replaced old ways of doing things. She applied this to her relationship with God and she understood that He would lift her up to Himself because she was too little to climb the rough stairway of perfection to reach Him. This is a point we will return to in our next chapter when we explore what love and littleness meant for Thérèse.

Like Francis, Thérèse interiorly enlightened by the Holy Spirit, was able to draw from ordinary sources eternal and life-giving Truths. She knew that it was the Spirit of Love Who purified her, enlightened her and set her aflame with His fire. Over and over again she prayed that she would be continuously set on fire until she was totally and unceasingly consumed by Love, until she died of love. This is the passionate language of loving union: longing, desire, thirst, consummation and union in the mutual embrace of love. All of these are present in the writings of Thérèse. 'I thirst for Love, fulfil my hope. Lord, make Your Divine Fire grow within me ... The more I feel it burning within me, the more my soul desires You.'[52] This was a journey of a lifetime but like all journeys there are key moments and encounters that usher in new experiences and new depths of love and union.

We know that Thérèse longed to die of love. Like Francis, she was prepared, even desired, to die a martyr's death in mission territory, but realising this was not going to happen to her in the physical sense of giving her life for Christ, she longed and prayed that she would die of love. This prayer was answered but it was not in an ecstatic sense of being carried off in transports of love. Thérèse, like Francis, realised towards the end of her life that hers would be a death of love, a martyrdom of love, simply because she followed closely in the footsteps of Jesus Crucified. Therefore if He answered her prayer to become like Him and to resemble Him in all things, then her death too would be a reflection of the totality and excess of love, so that even in the midst of seeming abandonment, pain and suffering she, like Jesus, would die a beautiful death of love in total self-abandonment. This abandonment she describes as the fruit of love, which will bring her into the arms of Jesus. She prepared her sisters for this, saying quite simply that this is the Gospel way, implying that they ought not to be disappointed or surprised by the reality of what might be a death agony, during which her heart would still sing interiorly a canticle of love. Thérèse knew that this sounded like foolishness to the worldly wise. 'Living on love, what strange folly! The world says to me, "Ah, stop your singing"',[53] but Thérèse wanted to go on singing that she was dying of love.

Even in death Thérèse wanted to continue to make Jesus known and loved. We are familiar with her desire to spend her heaven doing good on earth. However, in the context of love, Thérèse again used the image of

Fire and flame to describe this mission, which she knew had its source in God. 'You put this Fire of Heaven in my soul. I also want to spread its intense heat ... To carry your Fire far and wide.'[54] Her prayer was answered and her mission continues.

One Theresian scholar, Father Marie-Eugene of the Child Jesus associates Thérèse's spiritual motherhood with the wound of love she received when she was making the Way of the Cross. She relates that it was a few days after she made her Oblation to Merciful Love and she was so overwhelmed by the intensity of the flame of God's love that she felt she would die if it had lasted a moment longer. Reflecting on this, Fr. Marie-Eugene believes that Thérèse had reached the stage of transforming union, which he says is the wound of spiritual motherhood and it was, for Thérèse, her departure point for the transmission of her doctrine of Spiritual Childhood.[55] We will explore this teaching on littleness in our next Chapter.

Francis and Thérèse: Troubadours of Love

The lives of Francis and Thérèse are Canticles of Love. They are singers of the new song that witness to the primacy of love. In both lives this love has been described as Seraphic 'kindling them and firing them to their own heat, and wholly purifying them by a burning and all consuming flame'.[56] In both Francis and Thérèse, we see Who God can be and what He can do when a person surrenders completely by giving love in return for love. Yet each does this with a particularity that is unrepeatable. Such is the unique vocation of every person.

The *Canticle of Creatures*, written by Francis at the end of his life, is testimony to the experience of the glory of the Risen Christ, which Francis sees in a world that is ablaze with the glory of God. And Francis knew from within that he was caught up in this stupendous mystery of love at the heart of all creation and he asked the brothers to sing this canticle with him. Towards the end of her life, Thérèse wrote her Autobiography, which consists of three manuscripts, each of which end with the word 'love'. This is her Canticle to the Merciful Love of God, a love that is unconditional, tender, merciful and all consuming. The convent chaplain, Abbe Youf, described Thérèse as 'une ame chantante' — 'a singing soul', and most of her poetry was written to be sung to popular tunes, either at recreation or during common work such as when the sisters gathered to do the laundry. She literally did spread music and joy around her in these simple ways, while also disseminating her insights. This is even more striking when one remembers that St Teresa did not permit any singing in the Divine Office, which had to be recited on a monotone.

While on earth Francis and Thérèse suffered because Love was not loved. Their mission continues to make Love loved. The question is: how can one respond to such amazing love? Of oneself it is impossible, but with God all things are possible and the result is the consuming desire to live for love and to die for love because love is repaid by love alone. This is certainly evident in the lives of Francis and Thérèse. Both desired to resemble Jesus as perfectly as possible during their earthly lives and if possible to die a martyr's death in the flesh for love of Him. However, both came to understand by Divine illumination that

it is possible to die a martyr's death by being transformed by Love in the depths of one's being in the
ordinary circumstances of a very ordinary life. It is to
this extraordinary loving in the ordinary circumstances
of life that we will now turn, concentrating on the
mystery of love and littleness in our relationship with
God.

Reflection

How might Francis and Thérèse challenge you to be
more loving, creative and daring in your unique
following of Jesus?

Notes

[1] R. J. Armstrong, OFMCap., W. J. A. Hellmann, OFMConv., W.J.
     Short, OFM., *Francis of Assisi The Founder Early Documents*, vol.
     II, (London, New York: New City Press, 2000), p. 373.

[2] Carmel of Kilmacud, *Thoughts of the Servant of God Thérèse of
     the Child Jesus*, (P.J. Kenedy & Sons, USA: The Plimpton Press,
     1914), p. 1.

[3] R. J. Armstrong, OFMCap., W. J. A. Hellmann, OFMConv.,
     W.J. Short, OFM., *Francis of Assisi The Saint Early Documents*,
     vol. I, (London, New York: New City Press, 2000), pp. 82–6.

[4] *Ibid.*, p. 82.

[5] Armstrong *et al.*, *Francis of Assisi The Founder*, vol. II, p. 249.

[6] Armstrong *et al.*, *Francis of Assisi The Saint*, vol. I, p. 251.

[7] *Ibid.*, p. 42.

[8] *Ibid.*, p. 109.

[9] T. Matura, OFM., 'My Holy Father', in *Greyfriars Review*, 1/1,
     (USA: St Bonaventure University, 1987), p. 120.

[10] Armstrong *et al.*, *Francis of Assis The Founder*, vol. II, p. 631.

[11] Armstrong *et al.*, *Francis of Assisi The Saint*, vol. I, p. 128.

[12] *Ibid.*, p. 283.

13   *Ibid.,* p. 128.

14   *Ibid.,* pp. 139–157.

15   *Ibid.,* p. 84.

16   *Ibid.,* pp. 116–121.

17   Armstrong *et al., Francis of Assisi The Founder,* vol. II, p. 526.

18   *Ibid.,* pp. 632–3.

19   *Ibid.,* p. 632.

20   Armstrong *et al., Francis of Assisi The Saint,* vol. I, p. 186.

21   *Ibid.,* p. 105.

22   *Ibid.,* p. 79.

23   *Ibid.,* p. 120.

24   Armstrong *et al., Francis of Assisi The Founder,* vol. II, p. 386.

25   Armstrong *et al., Francis of Assisi The Saint,* vol. I, p. 122.

26   R. J. Armstrong, OFMCap., *St Francis of Assisi Writings for a Gospel Life,* (UK: St Pauls, 1994), p. 226.

27   J. Clarke, *Story of a Soul The Autobiography of St Thérèse of Lisieux,* (Washington DC: ICS Publications, 1972), p. 42.

28   *Ibid.,* p. 35.

29   *Ibid.,* p. 48.

30   *Ibid.,* p. 161.

31   Carmel of Kilmacud, *Thoughts of the Servant of God Thérèse of the Child Jesus,* (P. J. Kenedy & Sons, USA: The Plimpton Press, 1914), p. 155.

32   *Ibid.,* p. 234.

33   Clarke, *Story of a Soul,* p. 97.

34   *Ibid.,* p. 276.

35   D. Kinney, ODC., (Trans) *The Poetry of Saint Thérèse of Lisieux,* (Washington DC: ICS Publication, 1995), pp. 89–90.

36   G. Gaucher, *John and Thérèse Flames of Love The Influence of St John of the Cross in the Life and Writings of StThérèse of Lisieux,* (New York: Alba House, The Society of St Paul. 1999), p. 52.

37   Gaucher, *John and Thérèse Flames of Love,* p. 52.

38   Clarke, *Story of a Soul,* p. 259.

39   *Ibid.,* p. 179.

40   *Ibid.,* pp. 256–7.

41   *Ibid.,* p. 174.

42   *Ibid.,* p. 239.

43 *Ibid.*, p. 221.

44 Carmel of Kilmacud, *Thoughts of the Servant of God Thérèse of the Child Jesus*, p. 8.

45 Kinney, *The Poetry of Saint Thérèse of Lisieux*, p. 112.

46 Clarke, *Story of a Soul*, p. 276.

47 P. Ahern, *Maurice and Thérèse The Story of a Love*, (London: Darton Longman Todd, 1999), p. 135.

48 Kinney, *The Poetry of Saint Thérèse of Lisieux*, p. 126.

49 Clarke, *Story of a Soul*, p. 83.

50 *Ibid.*, p. 148.

51 Clarke, *Story of a Soul*, p. 258.

52 Kinney, *The Poetry of Saint Thérèse of Lisieux*, p. 151.

53 *Ibid.*, p. 92.

54 *Ibid.*, p. 127.

55 Gaucher, *John and Thérèse Flames of Love*, p. 123.

56 L. Colgan, 'The Meaning of Seraphic: Bonaventure and Francis, The Celestial Hierarch: Pseudo-Dionysius', in *The Cord*, 37/3, (USA: St Bonaventure University, 1987), p .74.

Chapter 7

Love and Littleness

Let them be lesser ... grounded on the solid rock of true humility.[1]

St Francis

Holiness is not in such or such a practice; it consists in a disposition of the heart that makes us humble and little in the arms of God.[2]

St Thérèse

F rancis and Thérèse grew in their profound understanding of the nature of a love that expends itself, gives unconditionally and forever, bends down and lowers itself in unceasing self-emptying to identify with human beings and to invite a response. This they learned from Jesus who said: 'Learn from Me, for I am gentle and humble of heart' (Mt 11:29). This gentleness and humility became for Francis and Thérèse a way of life. It became a legacy we now recognise respectively as minority and littleness. In many ways these words are interchangeable, and it is because of this we place Francis and Thérèse side by side as they teach us, through love and littleness from their own experience, who we are and who God is.

Francis and Minority

The Franciscan family has always understood that minority/littleness is a core Gospel value, characterised by childlikeness and servanthood. Cherished by Francis, it was his desire that being a minor or lesser brother should remain an identifying characteristic of his followers and their Gospel way to God. Celano roots this insight and inspiration of Francis at the very beginning of his call to form a fraternity. He tells us that, on the occasion of its founding, Francis gave the Order its name, saying, 'I want this Fraternity to be called the Order of Lesser Brothers ... grounded on the solid rock of true humility'.[3] However, we also know that this identity was clarified over a period of time, because initially when Francis and a small number of brothers embraced the Gospel way of life, they were called 'Penitents from Assisi' and 'Poor Minors'.

There is no doubt that minority was a distinguishing feature of Francis and his followers from a very early date. We have written evidence of this in a Letter of Jacques de Vitry, a noted Church historian who lived at the time of Francis. In a Letter dated 1216, he described the followers of Francis as 'Lesser brothers and lesser sisters'. Personal vocation and identity takes time to evolve and this is what happened to Francis and his first followers. This also happens to us if we persevere in openness and receptivity to the promptings of grace and inspiration in fidelity to our unique call. I can identify with this process when I look at the history of my own Religious Congregation of Franciscan Sisters Minoress. Our founding Sisters were known initially as 'The Sisterhood of St Francis'. A little later they were known as 'Missionary Sisters of St Francis'. However, the founding charism gradually evolved and emerged as minority, hence our enduring identity as Franciscan Sisters Minoress.

After the death of Francis, one of his learned friars, St Bonaventure, having lived as a lesser brother himself for many years, when reflecting on the life and legacy of Francis, had this to say in his Evening Sermon to celebrate the feast of St Francis. 'Learn from me, that is, be meek and humble after my example. A person is meek by loving his brothers, humble by loving lowliness or "minority"'.[4] This choice to embrace minority and journey into littleness links Francis and Thérèse as kindred spirits in a unique way, which will unfold as the chapter progresses.

Childlikeness and servanthood: this is the face of minority as it is lived in relation to God and with our brothers and sisters. Childlikeness places us in the stance of a beloved child of the Father, receiving absolutely everything as gift from Him. Like a child dependent upon its parents to be loved into existence, we too are totally dependent upon God, our Father and Creator, lovingly brought into existence by Him, cherished, nurtured and sustained by Him at every moment until we come to fullness of life and love in Him by our total union with Jesus in the power of the Holy Spirit.

Christ Himself made childlikeness a condition for entry into the Kingdom, saying, 'In truth I tell you, unless you change and become like little children you will never enter the Kingdom of Heaven' (Mt 18:3). Commenting on this text in relation to Francis and minority, one Franciscan scholar, Julio Mico, observes that there are varying degrees of littleness, saying that the little child mentioned by St Matthew in the above text is nothing and has nothing. A child such as this is representative of those who are on the margins of society. In Francis's day these would be the very poor, those without a voice or influence, lepers and outcasts. Mico points out that Jesus invites us to become like this little child, implying that we have the choice to humble ourselves, as Jesus did, as Francis did. This is a process freely chosen.[5] Finally in another text of St Matthew's Gospel (18:5) there are those who welcome the little ones and serve them. Here we have the Gospel basis for living as minors, as little ones and servants.

Jesus specifically chooses a *little* child. Therefore, to be in relationship with God as a *little* child challenges us to accept our own nothingness apart from Him, and our complete dependence on God in an attitude of acceptance, loving trust, lowliness, contentment, confidence and joy—to name but a few. All of these became operative in Francis's relationship with God because he had a deep sense of being loved into life as the recipient of the lavish goodness and love of the Father. Therefore, there is a positive attitude here that brings freedom and joy to those who embrace it. With God we are loved and very precious and, with child-like wonder, Francis wants everyone to 'Love the Lord God Who has given and gives to each one of us our whole body, our whole soul and our whole life'.[6]

It follows that if the Lord is the Giver of life and of all good gifts throughout our life, then we are recipients of the generous and provident God from birth to death—and beyond death itself to fullness of life. Therefore Francis acknowledged that we are poor because there is nothing in this life that we can call our own, except sin. Perhaps this is why he so eagerly embraced poverty. It is essential that we too (in our radical poverty as contingent beings) remain childlike through an open and trusting confidence in the providence of a Father who loves us personally, unconditionally and forever, despite experiences that might appear otherwise to the worldly wise. Joyful acceptance of this truth is not as easy as it appears. The reality and consequences of this attitude will be unravelled as we ponder the life and Writings of Francis and his practical living out of the call to be little in everyday relationships, events and circumstances.

Such a stance will wage war on our pride, independence and innate selfishness. Eventually, if we respond, the truth will indeed set us free, making us eager to praise and thank God for His presence and power not only in our own individual lives, but also in the lives of our brothers and sisters. To love, appreciate, praise and give thanks to our Father God in this way involves a life-long journey. Therefore, we could say that in our relationship with God, minority is the recognition of the inner reality of our radical poverty as a human being and as a loved child, while humility is our joyful acceptance and expression of this in our daily living, and in our relationships as servants of one another.

Celano described Francis as 'The servant of God, small in stature, humble in attitude, and lesser by profession'.[7] This is the Gospel image of Francis who patterned himself on Christ who is Child of the Father within the Godhead. This is an awesome mystery in which each of us is invited to participate with hearts full of thanksgiving. We become a child of the Father in and through and with Christ the Beloved. Francis knows this and, when he addresses the Father, he appeals to Him by reminding Him of this truth. In commenting on this approach to the Father, Leonard Lehmann OFMCap, observes the psychological skill with which Francis prays.

> He is Your beloved Son. At His baptism and transfiguration on Mount Tabor You Yourself said that in Him You were well pleased. He is the one Who ever suffices You in every regard; that is, Who was perfectly obedient. Through Him You have given us so much. May he now offer You thanksgiving on our behalf, since we ourselves are not able to do so.[8]

The psychological skill mentioned by Lehmann is surely based on the filial confidence and trust Francis had in his loving Father. Even at the very beginning of his vocation when he met Pope Innocent III to seek approval for his way of life, Francis showed how deep his trust was and where it was founded. When the Pope expressed his misgivings because of the many hardships involved in the step Francis desired to take,

Francis replied, 'My Lord, I trust in my Lord Jesus Christ. Since He has promised to give us life and glory in heaven, he will not deprive us of our bodily necessities when we need them on earth'.⁹ When the Pope eventually approved the Rule, Francis was overjoyed and he continued to grow each day in deeper trust, encouraging his brothers to have great confidence in the Divine Mercy. This foundation of filial trust and confidence gave Francis boldness of approach in the presence not only of Popes and Prelates, but also in the presence of God Himself—a daring trust and confidence we also see in Thérèse in similar circumstances.

Being the beloved child of the extravagant love of the Father involves a loving response in imitation of Christ, 'Who, being in the form of God, did not count equality with God something to be grasped. But he emptied Himself, taking the form of a slave, becoming as human beings are' (Ph 2:6–7). Francis recognised the innate human tendency to grasp whatever gives status, dignity, superiority and domination. He named it as appropriation, that is, calling our own that which does not belong to us and taking glory that belongs to God alone. The opposite tendency to grasping and appropriation is poverty, the recognition that we live in the world of gift. The way in which Francis starkly contrasts the grasping and the poverty is most clearly described in his Twenty Eight Admonitions, which have been described as both 'A Canticle of Inner Poverty and as 'A Canticle of Minority', which shows just how inter-related and inter-dependent these two Gospel values are. In *A Salutation of the Virtues*, Francis called poverty and humility 'sisters'.¹⁰

In the *Admonitions* Francis clearly outlines how we manifest in the ordinary everyday situations of our lives whether we are being led in the way of minority by the Spirit of God or by our own selfishness. 'A servant of God can be known to have the Spirit of the Lord in this way: if, when the Lord performs some good through him, his flesh does not therefore exalt itself'.[11] Jesus reminds us, 'Anyone who exalts himself will be humbled and whoever humbles himself will be exalted' (Mt 23:12). Francis understood this teaching of Jesus and took it to heart, reminding his followers that they must not become proud if the Lord works some good through them, nor must they be jealous when He works through someone else. 'Whoever envies his brother the good that the Lord says or does in him incurs a sin of blasphemy because he envies the Most High Himself Who says and does every good thing'.[12]

Francis deeply understood his Lord and Master, Jesus Christ, who, when the rich young man asked Him about Eternal Life and addressed Him as 'Good Master', Jesus replied, 'Why do you call me good? No one is good but God alone' (Lk 18:18–19). Just as Jesus realised that God was the source of all goodness manifested in His life and ministry, so too Francis realised that God alone is Good and he alone is the source of all the good that Francis is empowered to do by His grace. Therefore he prayed, 'All-powerful, most holy, most high, supreme God: all good, supreme good, totally good, You Who alone are good, may we give You all praise, all glory, all thanks, all honour, all blessing and all good … Amen'.[13] It was from within his experience of the All-good God, revealed in Jesus Christ, the poor and humble One, that Francis learned to rejoice in his poverty and humbly acknowledge that in his emptiness he was capable of being filled with the fullness of God. Therefore, he had no desire to claim as his own what did not belong to him in any sphere of life, whether natural or spiritual. Everything comes from God: riches, talents, gifts, good looks, knowledge, wisdom and special charisms. Francis lists them all in his *Fifth Admonition*. We see how rooted he was in the very ordinary experiences of life and relationships where grace and nature manifest themselves.

Deeply conscious of his own frailty and weakness Francis did not rely on his own resources. He acknowledged his sinfulness publicly.

> I have offended the Lord God in many ways by my serious faults especially in not observing the Rule that I have promised Him and in not saying the Office as the Rule prescribes either out of negligence or by reason of my weakness or because I am ignorant or stupid.[14]

Towards the end of his life when his reputation for holiness was spreading and some people thought he was a saint, Francis realistically affirmed his total dependence on the grace of God, saying, 'Don't praise me as if I were safe; I can still have sons and daughters!'.[15] And on another occasion he wrote that it is God alone Who created us and saves us by His grace and mercy. Holiness is not our achievement. It is the mercy of God that reaches down to us in our poverty and littleness, a truth Thérèse also experienced and desired to teach as we shall see later.

Within the depths of our hearts, to really know and accept our poverty and God's lavishness, requires deep humility. Such inner awareness of the truth led Francis to adopt a humble stance not only before God but also among his brothers and sisters. This attitude is manifested in the way in which Francis refers to himself when he communicates in his written words, (his *Testament* and his Letters), but more especially in his relationships on a daily basis. In his *Testament*, Francis referred to himself as 'Little brother Francis, your servant'. In his *First Letter to the Custodians* he calls himself 'Brother Francis, your servant and little one in the Lord God'. We find an added dimension in his *Second Letter to Custodians*, where he describes himself as 'The least of the servants of God'. In his *Letter to Rulers of the Peoples* he is 'Brother Francis, your little and looked-down-upon servant', and finally in his *Second Letter to the Faithful* he is not only a brother and a servant but also a subject as well, 'Brother Francis, your servant and subject'.[16]

The spoken and written words were an outward expression of an inner attitude of littleness, which marked Francis as a servant of all. This is the other face of minority, which remains a distinctive characteristic of all who call themselves 'minor' after the example of Francis. This Gospel attitude is rooted in the example of Christ who became a servant. We have already reflected on the theme of 'The Suffering Servant' in Isaiah and the fulfilment of this prophecy in the redemptive suffering and death of Christ. In our present context of minority in everyday living we will see how, in very ordinary and familiar ways, love and littleness touch every aspect of life.

The idea of being a servant has connotations which our modern world would not easily relate to, or agree with. However, in the Biblical sense, the servant image is the mystery of an extravagant and vulnerable love, present among us in Jesus Christ, Who said, 'Here am I among you as one who serves' (Lk 22: 27).

We saw in the previous chapter that Jesus remains among us in self-emptying, self-giving love in the Eucharist. Here we are in the realm of profound mystery and it requires deep faith to embrace it, enter into it and make such a stance the foundation of our life. This is the only way to follow in the footsteps of Jesus, who taught us that true greatness lies in loving service of each other, especially in the little opportunities that ordinary life presents.

Francis addressed all the brothers as equals and he was insistent that every ministry and every type of work was a grace and should express the reality of being both brother and servant. Those who were placed in authority were reminded of the example of Jesus at the Last Supper. Francis learned well from the self-giving love and service of Jesus Who washed the feet of His disciples and asked them to follow His example. This Gospel text appears in the Rule of Life Francis wrote for his brothers, saying that they should be prepared to wash each other's feet.[17] The same teaching is repeated in the Admonitions. The text bears quoting in full.

> I did not come to be served, but to serve, says the Lord. Let those who are placed over others boast about that position as much as they would if they were assigned the duty of washing the feet of their brothers. And if they are more upset at having their place over others taken away from them than at losing their position at their feet, the more they store up a money bag to the peril of their soul.[18]

What Jesus and Francis are asking of us is very challenging. Essentially it means loving self-forgetfulness and self-sacrifice that always seeks to put the other person first. Francis gives very practical examples of how we may do this—at some cost to ourselves—as we radiate forgiveness, joy, peace and acceptance of one another. His *Rule* and *Admonitions* in particular, spell out this way of life with specific details. We will mention a few here to illustrate the concreteness with which Francis lived the Gospel message of love and littleness.

Francis encouraged the brothers to be true imitators of the servant Jesus, showing love by their deeds and example, especially when things go against them. In this context, Francis speaks of being hurt, being persecuted, being angry because of another's sin, being misjudged and having our good name or reputation taken away. All these examples from the *Admonitions* are ordinary, everyday experiences of living with others. Who among us has not been hurt by the words and actions of others, or who among us has not hurt others by our words and actions? Yet Francis repeats those words of Jesus in the Sermon on the Mount, saying, 'The Lord says: Love your enemies, do good to those who hate you and pray for those who persecute and slander you'.[19] Francis would have us act like this because of the love we have for God and showing that love by our deeds.

Again we may ask the question: who among us has not been angered by the sinful behaviour of another, or perhaps others have been angered by our sinful behaviour? Yet Francis is adamant that we must not usurp the place of God. We are not called to judge and condemn others. We are called to love. In his *Rule* he counselled the brothers to 'Be careful not to be angry or disturbed at the sin of another, for anger and disturbance impede charity in themselves and in others'.[20] According to the Franciscan scholar, Regis Armstrong, OFMCap., in Admonition Eleven, Francis takes this teaching a step further where he says, 'No matter how another person may sin, if a servant of God becomes disturbed and angry because of this and not because of charity, he is storming up guilt for himself'.[21] Armstrong suggests that a humble servant of God should avoid being angry at anything at all because it is possible for us to cling to our anger, to 'appropriate' or own it in a way that lords it over or manipulates others. To live without anger or upset, two seemingly natural reactions that we would see as psychologically healthy to express, is to live justly and without anything of our own.[22] This is a radical way to live in love and littleness. Love is central; anger is not. We find this repeated in the Twenty Seventh Admonition where Francis says: 'Where there is patience and humility, there is neither anger nor disturbance'.[23]

Who among us has not suffered the humiliation of not living up to our own expectations or the expectations of others? Rightly or wrongly, perhaps our good name or reputation has been harmed or sullied. In such situations, the reality of our virtue will become clear in our response. Francis says that even though we make take upon ourselves much prayer, penance and other obligations, when the time of testing comes, 'They are immediately offended and disturbed about a single word which seems harmful to their bodies or about something which might be taken away from them'.[24] He is insistent that we have as much patience and humility as we show in those trying times. Always with Francis there is the realisation that if we walk in the footsteps of the poor and humble Christ, we will give our very selves away in love as He did. We will cling to nothing, either spiritual or material, and yet in Him we have everything. He is all our riches. He is enough for us if we allow him to be.

Jesus said, 'In all truth I tell you, by himself the Son can do nothing' (Jn 5:19). As Son of the Father he receives everything from the Father as a little child does. The same is true for us. This is what it means to be a lesser brother or sister, to walk with extraordinary love and littleness in the ups and downs of daily life and relationships, bearing hardships patiently and cheerfully for the sake of love. Francis describes how this Gospel attitude is embodied in the minor brother or sister.

> The Brothers and Sisters should be meek, peaceful and unassuming, gentle and humble, speaking courteously to everyone, as is right. Wherever they are and wherever they go in the world, they are not to quarrel, get into arguments or condemn others. Rather they should show that they are joyful in the Lord, good humoured and gracious, as is right. When they greet others they should say: The Lord give you peace.[25]

Francis died as he had lived. Owning nothing, appropriating nothing, he desired to be placed naked on the naked earth, to be clothed with the 'New Man' (cf. Ep 4:22–24) recreated in Christ Jesus, his God and his All.

Thérèse and The Little Way of Spiritual Childhood

Like Francis, it took time for Thérèse to grow into the fullness of her identity as her 'Little Way' evolved and matured. She was always attracted by littleness. Recalling the day when at a very young age she asked her father's permission to enter Carmel, Thérèse, her father's '*little* Queen' writes of a sacred memory that was 'a symbolic action'. Her father went to a low wall and plucked a little white flower together with the root and gave it to her, explaining how God brought it into being and preserved it. Thérèse said it was like hearing her own story, 'So great was the resemblance between what Jesus had done for *the little flower* and *little Thérèse*'.[26] This memory must have made a lasting impression because when Thérèse was in Carmel, writing her memoirs, she referred to herself as the little flower of Jesus and also as the Blessed Virgin's little flower.

Countless numbers of times Thérèse speaks of littleness as she experienced it in the Person of Jesus Christ and within herself in her relationship to God. Our interest here is the way in which Thérèse gradually became aware of her special vocation and mission to pave a Gospel path for herself and others to follow, a way that gave love a special childlike quality of littleness, a way which she describes as, 'A little way, a way that is very straight, very short, and totally new'.[27] When she described it thus, it was in the context of her felt inability to climb the steep stairway of perfection. Though she felt called to greatness it was not in the sense of following in the footsteps of those saints who were renowned for heroic works, severe penances and great mystical experiences. Compared to them, Thérèse said it was like the difference that exists between a mountain summit and a little grain of sand. And yet, Thérèse knew in her heart that she was called to be a great saint—but in a little way. This has made all the difference, and continues to inspire and give hope to all who experience the paradox of their utter powerlessness and their great desires for holiness. When she tried to express these desires to a Jesuit priest, Laurent Blino, he was scandalised by her audacity, which he felt bordered on presumption.

Thérèse did not feel understood or free until a Franciscan priest, Alexis Prou, set her full sail on the way of confidence and trust. (It is interesting in our present context that the priest was a follower of St Francis!) Her own words bear witness to this turning point in her journey:

> After speaking only a few words, I was understood in a marvellous way and my soul was like a book in which this priest read better than I did myself. He launched me full sail upon the waves of confidence and love which so strongly attracted me, but upon which I dared not advance.[28]

A child loves. A child trusts. A child has confidence. It was in relating to God as a very little child that Thérèse learned how to deal with her weakness and powerlessness. Yet even in this she had to learn that there are degrees of littleness and differing attitudes and responses to being little. Like most of us who earnestly seek to love God, we strive by our own efforts to do His will and to please Him. This is good and it is part of the journey and the developing relationship. However, at some point on our journey, like Francis and Thérèse, we realise the truth of St John's words mentioned in the previous chapter, that it is not our love for God but God's love for us that is the amazing revelation.

From childhood Thérèse had tried to prove how much she loved God. She offered little prayers and sacrifices at great cost to herself. According to her own records, when she was preparing for her First Holy Communion, she offered God 1,949 sacrifices and 2,773 short prayers. Was this the result of belonging to a business family where daily earning was significant and had effects on the wellbeing of the family? According to the Theresian scholar, Conrad de Meester, being the child of business entrepreneurs did influence the Martin sisters, and Thérèse in particular. Marked by the constant preoccupation with earning, saving and recounting everything of monetary value, was carried over into the spiritual sphere.[29] As De Meester points out, such an atmosphere nurtured a Do-It-Yourself type of spirituality that makes one feel self-sufficient. It also nurtured a sense of justice and the weighing up of spiritual merits at the great Judgement Day. Thérèse made this link for herself on the occasion of Prize Giving day at home. Describing those times when she received rewards for succeeding in her studies, she said, 'My heart was beating rapidly as I received my prizes and the crown. It was like a picture of the Last Judgment'.[30] It is interesting that Francis also came from a merchant background where profit and loss, achievement and striving, earning and merit played a part. Yet both Francis and Thérèse eventually left this way of thinking and acting behind, as they entered more deeply in the world of God's amazing love where all is gift, all is given, and they experienced that the other face of justice is mercy.

Initially both Francis and Thérèse were ardent in seeking to *do* all in their power to love God and please Him. We too can have an attitude of 'Lord, what do You want me to *do* ?', rather than 'Lord, who do You want me to *be*?'. Perhaps this is a natural and progressive journey until being and doing are integrated in one great act of love. We dispense with neither, but the emphasis changes. Certainly when Thérèse entered Carmel, she was intent on doing everything in her power to show her love for God. She tried not to let any opportunity pass, however small, which would prove her love for God and save souls for Him. Even in the midst of suffering, grief and desolation Thérèse could say, 'I accept everything out of love for You'.[31] Eventually, as happens in our lives too, there is a shift in emphasis and we realise that our love for God pales to nothing in comparison with His extravagant love, which longs to give itself completely to us as a gift. In that maturing process, Thérèse learned a very valuable lesson, a lesson that was partially revealed to her when she received her 'Christmas conversion grace', namely that God can do in an instant what we are unable to do even after many years of effort and striving. However, like all revelations and mysteries of God, there is always a greater depth of understanding to be explored and experienced, and Thérèse's discovery of her Little Way illustrates this very clearly.

Reminiscent of Francis and his deep knowledge of his own weakness and sinfulness, Thérèse too admits that even after many years in Carmel, she was not the 'perfect' religious sister. After six years in Carmel, Thérèse had this to say, 'Now I am astonished at nothing. I am not disturbed at seeing myself weakness itself. On the contrary, it is in my weakness that I glory, and I expect each day to discover new imperfections in myself'.[32] She relates that she fell asleep during prayer and thanksgiving after Holy Communion. During times of sickness and debilitation she was unable to pray the Divine Office. In the infirmary she was sometimes tearful, irritable and impatient. Yet on her deathbed she could say, 'O how happy I am to see myself imperfect and to be in need of God's mercy so much, even at the moment of my death'.[33] Where had Thérèse learned such wisdom and what lay behind her self-knowledge and joyful self-acceptance? To answer that question we have to return to her experience of maturing in her understanding of littleness.

Having received encouragement in the words of Fr Alexis to set sail on the way of confidence and trust, Thérèse, despite a sense of her own incapacity and powerlessness, or more precisely because of it, she entered a new phase in her relationship with God. She was still very much aware of the existing gap between her desire to become a great saint and the realisation of this desire, but she adhered steadfastly to her desire and asserted that she would not give in to discouragement. She reasoned that if God gave her such desires, then it must be possible for her to be a great saint, even in her littleness. She continued to struggle, as we all have to, with the reality of our constant weaknesses, failures and imperfections. We know of her dilemma because she tells us:

> To grow is impossible for me; I must endure myself such as I am with all my imperfections, but I do want to find a means of going to heaven by a little path that is very straight and very short; an entirely new little path.[34]

Thérèse searched for her new little path in the word of God. A few texts in particular are very significant. The first was a text she found in the Notebook that her sister, Celine, brought to Carmel with her and to which Thérèse had access. What she read there filled her with delight: 'Whoever is a little one, let him come to me' (Pr 9: 4). Thérèse felt she had found what she was searching for, but she sought further enlightenment and was overjoyed to find the following text: 'As one whom a mother caresses, so I will comfort you; you shall be carried at the breasts, and upon the knees they shall caress you' (Is 66:13, 12). With such a revelation from the Word of God, Thérèse exclaimed:

> Ah! Never did words more tender and more melodious come to give joy to my soul. The elevator which must raise me to heaven is Your arms, O Jesus! And for this I had no need to grow up, but rather I had to remain little and become this more and more'.[35]

This is a remarkable insight for Thérèse and it was the beginning of her Little Way. The arms of Jesus would be her 'spiritual elevator' to take her into the heart of God. At last she realised that her helplessness was not an obstacle. To remain little and become so, more and more, was actually an invitation from God Himself. No wonder Thérèse could say: 'O my God, You have surpassed all my expectations, I want only to sing of Your Mercies'.[36] Thérèse had discovered in that instant what many of us take a lifetime to discover, namely, that God in His great and tender mercy lovingly stoops down and picks us up as only God can. All He asks is our desire to be the child in His arms, close to His heart and responding with total love and absolute trust. In other words we allow God to love us and to do for us what we cannot do for ourselves. This is His heart's desire. Union with Him is a gift, His gift, and He comes to meet us where *we* are. He is the One who condescendingly bends down to us in our lowliness and littleness and lifts us up. Such overwhelming love is difficult for us to believe in and accept, but when we do, there is freedom and joy and peace, as Jesus promised.

Love that is essentially merciful was the great discovery that led Thérèse into a new phase in her relationship with God, and a new understanding and acceptance of herself in all her perceived inadequacies and powerlessness. Thérèse had tried very hard to correct her faults and failings but she gradually realised that she was striving for the impossible. However, with grace and new insights into the mystery of God's love and dealings with her, she could now accept the frailty of her humanity and surrender it to the merciful love of God, like a little child in its mother's arms. Thérèse realised that she was being invited to a new depth of detachment and surrender. In a letter to Celine, Thérèse admits that her heart is not entirely empty of herself. Therefore, all self pre-occupation, even in spiritual matters, must be surrendered in trust and confidence in order to become totally receptive to the merciful love of God.

In this purifying and transforming process, it becomes obvious that Jesus, not Thérèse is the centre of attention. 'The "I-You" relationship underwent an inversion and became "You-I". The determined attitude of "I want to do it and I want to do it for You" became much more peaceful and trusting'.[37] Thérèse now understood the importance of being totally open and receptive to God's gift of Himself and what He wanted to do within her. She writes: 'Merit does not consist in doing or in giving much, but rather in receiving, in loving much'.[38]

All Thérèse had to do was to surrender herself with absolute trust and confidence into the arms of God. What she could not do for herself, God would do for her, and in her, and through her. She uses a number of images to illustrate this revelation. We have already referred to her comparison of the elevator and the arms of Jesus, which will lift her effortlessly up to God. She also uses the image of the eagle and the little bird saying that she sees herself not as an eagle but as a weak little fledgling, yet she admits that she has the eyes and heart of an eagle. She sees the great saints, the eagles, flying to the heart of the Trinity but she is unable to fly. It is not within her power. All she can do is flap her wings while keeping her eyes steadily on the Divine Sun. As she develops this image, she is convinced that the little bird will not be troubled by its extreme weakness and powerlessness. Rather with bold surrender Thérèse has daring trust and utter confidence in God's love for her, which 'reaches unto folly'. Therefore she concludes, 'Jesus, I am too little to perform great actions, and my own folly is this: to trust that Your love will accept me as Your victim'. Thus she can fly to the Sun of Love 'with the Divine Eagle's own wings'.[39] Consequently when she offers herself as a victim to God's Merciful Love, Thérèse understands that God Himself will be her sanctity. Like Francis, with utter confidence she appeals to the Father through Jesus, saying:

> Since You loved me so much as to give me Your only Son as my Saviour and my Spouse, the infinite treasures of His merits are mine. I offer them to You with gladness, begging You to look upon me only in the Face of Jesus and in His heart burning with love'.[40]

Again, like Francis being placed naked on the naked earth before meeting Sister Death, so too Thérèse, in the evening of her life, is happy to come before God with empty hands. Thérèse has matured and all she desires now is to allow God to fill her emptiness. Therefore she opens herself unreservedly to the infinite love and tenderness pent up in the heart of God asking that it may overflow into her soul. She now understands that this overflow of infinite love, tenderness and mercy must also overflow in her life with her brothers and sisters. Nurtured as she was on the Word of God, we know Thérèse understood at ever greater depth the call to live the great Commandment of love. Her new insights into the overflowing of God's love into her own heart reflects another teaching of Jesus where He said, 'Give and there will be gifts for you: a full measure, pressed down, shaken together and overflowing, will be poured into your lap' (Lk.6: 38). Jesus said this in the context of compassionate loving, where judgement and condemnation have no place. This is possible because, as Thérèse experienced, 'It is no longer I who live, but Christ lives in me'.(Ga 2:20).

With penetrating insight and awareness, Thérèse touches the hearts of her sisters in community by loving service in the smallest and most ordinary circumstances of life. Everything is of value. All is grace. Nothing is outside the realm of love and mercy. Like Francis she is a very little sister and servant in ways that can be understood and lived by every person who desires to follow in the footprints of Christ, Child and Servant of God, and in this Thérèse models herself on the humble Virgin of Nazareth.

> It's you make me feel it really can be done
> To follow you, O Queen of all the Saints! …
> In daily little things I see the path you tread.
> O Mary, next to you, I love my staying small;
> …Your Visitation to your Cousin I recall
> And learn to imitate your ardent charity.[41]

Thérèse knew that her 'Little Way' is all confidence and love and she teaches that we can never have too much confidence in the mercy and love of God.

Francis and Thérèse: Always in Relationship

Francis and Thérèse always lived in relationship, and from our reflections in this chapter on love and littleness, three areas of relationship become obvious: God, others and themselves. Both Francis and Thérèse experienced their inner poverty before God. In this relationship God is seen as a generous and provident Father whose extravagant and exquisitely tender and merciful love is lavished on His children in Jesus Christ, through the power of the Holy Spirit. As recipients of this amazing love, reaching down to the weakness of a little child, Francis and Thérèse experienced themselves as poor, dependent, vulnerable children, totally trusting in, and entrusting themselves to, Infinite Love. Realising their own weakness, powerlessness and dependency, Francis and Thérèse reached out and accepted others with the same tender, merciful and steadfast love that they experienced in the heart of God.

Relationship with others is at the heart of the way of minority as lived by Francis, who came among us as a lesser little brother and servant. Relationship is at the heart of The Little Way of Spiritual Childhood lived by Thérèse, who came among us as a little child running a giant's course in the way of love and littleness. The lives of both are embodied in their Prayers and Writings, yet their personal example speaks more loudly than words ever could, as they invite us to travel their Gospel path. Accepting such an invitation will surely challenge many of our present ways of relating to God, others and ourselves. May they accompany us on our journey as brother and sister. As companions and friends may they teach us by words and example how we too, can sing our new song to the delight and joy of the heart of God, who taught us that true greatness lies in littleness.

Francis and Thérèse desire to be in relationship with us too. After his death, the brothers knew Francis was still in their midst. 'Crowned with honour and glory

... he stands by the throne of God, devoted to dealing effectively with the concerns of those he left on earth'.[42] And we cannot forget the conversation Thérèse had on her deathbed, when a sister said to her, 'You will look down from the heights of Heaven, will you not?'. Thérèse replied, '"No, I shall come down"'.[43] Can we doubt their presence with us, and their powerful intercession on our behalf?

I will leave the last words to our two great 'little' saints. Francis said, 'I have done what was mine to do. May Christ teach you what is yours to do',[44] and Thérèse said, 'I feel that if You found a soul weaker and littler than mine, which is impossible, You would be pleased to grant it still greater favours, provided it abandoned itself with total confidence to Your Infinite Mercy'.[45]

Could this little soul be me? Could it be you? With a grateful heart and with childlike trust, abandonment and confidence, let us do what is ours to do—now!

Reflection

What would you like to say to Francis and Thérèse at the end of this Gospel journey with them?

Notes

1   R. J. Armstrong, OFMCap., W. J. A. Hellmann, OFMConv., W. J. Short, OFM., *Francis of Assisi The Saint Early Documents*, vol. I, (London, New York: New City Press, 2000), p. 217.

2   C. De Meester, OCD., *The Power of Confidence. Genesis and Structure of the Way of Spiritual Childhood of St Thérèse of Lisieux*, (USA: Society of St Paul, 1998), p. 227.

3   R. J. Armstrong *et al.*, *Francis of Assisi The Saint*, vol. I, p. 217.

4   R. J. Armstrong, OFMCap., W. J. A. Hellmann, OFMConv., W. J. Short, OFM., *Francis of Assisi The Founder Early Documents,* vol. II, (London, New York: New City Press, 2000), p. 517.

5   J. Mico, OFMCap., 'The Spirituality of St Francis: Minority', Translated by P. Barratt, OFMCap., in *Greyfriars Review,* 9/2, (USA: The Franciscan Institute, St Bonaventure University, 1995), pp. 125–145.

6   Armstrong *et al., Francis of Assisi The Saint,* vol. I, p. 84.

7   Armstrong *et al., Francis of Assisi The Founder,* vol. II, p. 256.

8   L. Lehmann, OFMCap., 'We Thank You: The Structure and Content of Chapter 23 of the Earlier Rule', in *Greyfriars Review,* 5/1, (USA: St Bonaventure University, 1991), pp.1–54.

9   Armstrong *et al., Francis of Assisi. The Founder,* vol. II, p. 50.

10 Armstrong *et al., Francis of Assisi The Saint,* vol. 1, p.164.

11 *Ibid.,* p. 133.

12 *Ibid.,* p. 132.

13 *Ibid.,* p. 162.

14 *Ibid.,* p. 119.

15 Armstrong *et al., Francis of Assisi The Founder,* vol. II, p. 333.

16 Armstrong *et al., Francis of Assisi The Saint,* vol. 1 p. 124, p. 56, p. 58, p. 45.

17 *Ibid.,* p. 68.

18 *Ibid.,* p. 130.

19 *Ibid.,* p. 132.

20 *Ibid.,* p. 104.

21 *Ibid.,* p. 133.

22 R. J. Armstrong, OFMCap., 'The Prophetic Implications of the Admonitions', *Laurentianum,* vol. 26, (USA: The Franciscan Institute, St Bonaventure University, 1985), pp. 902–931.

23 Armstrong *et al., Francis of Assisi The Saint,* vol. I, p. 136.

24 *Ibid.,* p. 133.

25 TOR Rule, Article 20.

26 J. Clarke, OCD., *Story of a Soul The Autobiography of St Thérèse of Lisieux,* (Washington DC: ICS Publications, 1972), p. 108.

27 *Ibid.,* p. 207.

28 *Ibid.,* pp. 173–4.

29 C. De Meester, *With Empty Hands The Message of Thérèse of Lisieux*, (London, New York: Burns & Oates, A Continuum Imprint, 2002), p. 43.

30 Clarke, *Story of a Soul*, p. 45.

31 *Ibid.*, p. 217.

32 *Ibid.*, p. 224.

33 *Ibid.*, p. 267.

34 *Ibid.* ,p. 207.

35 *Ibid.*, p. 208.

36 *Ibid.*, p. 208.

37 De Meester, *With Empty Hands The Message of Thérèse of Lisieux*, p. 50.

38 *Ibid.*, p. 53.

39 Clarke, *Story of a Soul*, pp. 199–200.

40 *Ibid.*, p. 276.

41 A. Bancroft, (Trans) *Poems of St Thérèse of Lisieux*, (London: Harper Collins, 1996), p. 173.

42 Armstrong *et al.*, *Francis of Assisi The Saint*, vol. I, p. 288.

43 Carmel of Kilmacud, *Thoughts of the Servant of God Thérèse of the Child Jesus*, (P.J.Kenedy & Sons, USA: The Plimpton Press, 1914). p. 210.

44 Armstrong *et al.*, *Francis of Assisi The Founder*, vol. II, p. 386.

45 *Clark, Story of a Soul*, p. 200.

Conclusion

Great 'Little' Saints

Praised be You, my Lord, through our Sister Bodily Death, from whom no one living can escape. ... Blessed are those whom death will find in Your most holy will.[1]

St Francis

I am not dying, I am entering into life ... Believe that I shall be your true little sister for all eternity.[2]

St Thérèse

W e have now come full circle. We began this book with the natural birth and natural childhood of Francis of Assisi and Thérèse of Lisieux, and we have ended with their spiritual birth and spiritual childhood, marking them as great 'little' Saints who are willing to journey with us in the adventure of love and littleness.

Both Francis and Thérèse knew that they had a mission to others. Their vocation was not for themselves alone. Within the mystery of Divine Providence and Divine condescension their spirit lives on and their message and mission is universally known and loved. They have shown us how to be a child of God and a brother and sister to all. Their particular charism within the Church is marked by love and littleness and both gave a particular stamp of originality to its expression. Nevertheless, in both we see a profound consciousness of the way in which God has come among us in lowliness, bending down to us with amazing love in the incomprehensible mystery of littleness, marked by selfless love and humble service.

Distinguished by self-forgetful love, which gives itself totally to the Beloved, Francis and Thérèse became pure capacity for God, realising that He desires to give himself to us even more intensely and completely than we desire to give ourselves to Him. Yet, there is mutuality in love; therefore Francis could say, 'Hold back nothing of yourselves for yourselves, that He who gives Himself totally to you may receive you totally!'.[3] In a similar vein, Thérèse writes, 'It is said it is much sweeter to give rather than to receive, and it is true. But when Jesus wills to take for Himself the sweetness of giving, it would not be gracious to refuse. Let us allow Him to take and give all He wills.

Perfection consists in doing his will'.[4] And this she did with the utmost confidence and trust.

At the end of this particular stage of our journey with Francis and Thérèse, are not our hearts filled with praise and gratitude to the Father for revealing to us, through His Beloved Son Jesus, and in Him, through Francis and Thérèse, the tremendous adventure that is ours when we welcome God into our lives with childlike love and absolute trust and confidence?. Therefore, with Jesus, and filled with joy by the Holy Spirit, we pray: 'I bless you, Father, Lord of heaven and of earth, for hiding these things from the learned and the clever and revealing them to little children. Yes, Father, for that is what it has pleased You to do' (Lk 10: 21). May we be counted among those little ones.

Notes

[1]   R. J. Armstrong, OFMCap., W. J. A. Hellmann, OFMConv., W. J. Short, OFM., *Francis of Assisi The Saint Early Documents,* vol. I, (London, New York: New City Press, 2000), p. 114.

[2]   P. Ahern, *Maurice and Thérèse The Story of a Love,* (London: Darton Longman & Todd, 1999), pp. 130, 169.

[3]   Armstrong *et al, Francis of Assisi The Saint Early Documents,* vol. I, p. 118.

[4]   C. De Meester, *With Empty Hands The Message of Thérèse of Lisieux,* (London, New York: Burns & Oates. A Continuum Imprint, 2002), p. 53.

Bibliography

Ahern, P., *Maurice and Thérèse: The Story of a Love*. London: Darton, Longman & Todd, 1999.

Armstrong OFMCap, R. J. (editor and translator), *Clare of Assisi: Early Documents*. NY: Paulist Press, 1988.

Armstrong OFMCap, R. J., *St Francis of Assisi. Writings for a Gospel Life*. UK: St Pauls, 1994.

Armstrong OFMCap, R. J., Hellmann OFMConv, W. J. A., Short OFM, W. J. , *Francis Of Assisi The Founder Early Documents*. vol. I. London, New York: New City Press, 2000.

Armstrong OFMCap, R. J., Hellmann OFMConv, W. J. A., Short OFM, W. J., *Francis Of Assis The Founder Early Documents*. vol. II. London, New York: New City Press, 2000.

Balthasar von, H. U., *Two Sisters in the Spirit: Thérèse of Lisieux and Elizabeth of the Trinity*. San Francisco: Ignatius Press, 1992.

Bancroft, A., *St Thérèse of Lisieux: Poems*. London: Fount. Harper Collins, 1996.

Benedict XVI, Pope, *Spe Salvi*. Roma, 2007.

Benedict XVI , Pope, *Verbum Domini. Post-Synodal Exhortation on the Word of God*. London: CTS, 2010.

Bergstrom-Allen, J. & McGreal, W. (eds.), *The Gospel Sustains Me: The Word of God in the Life and Love of Saint Thérèse of Lisieux*. St Albert Press & Edizioni Carmelitane, 2009.

Carmel of Kilmacud, *Thoughts of the Servant of God Thérèse of the Child Jesus*. New York: P. J. Kennedy & Sons, USA: The Plimpton Press, 1914.

Clarke OCD, J. (trans.), *Story of a Soul: The Autobiography of St Thérèse of Lisieux.* Washington D.C.: ICS Publication, 1976.

Clarke OCD, J. , *St Thérèse of Lisieux: General Correspondence.* vol. II. Washington, D.C: ICS Publications, 1988.

De Meester OCD, C., *The Power of Confidence: Genesis and Structure of the Way of Spiritual Childhood of St Thérèse of Lisieux.* USA: Society of St Paul, 1998.

De Meester OCD, C., *With Empty Hands: The Message of Thérèse of Lisieux.* London, New York: Burns & Oates. A Continuum Imprint, 2002.

Descouvemont, P., (text), Loose, H. N., (Photographs), *Thérèse and Lisieux,* Canada: Novalis, Grand Rapids, MI: Eerdmans, Dublin: Veritas, 1996.

Gaucher, G., *The Spiritual Journey of Thérèse of Lisieux.* London: Darton, Longman and Todd, 1987.

Gaucher, G., *John and Thérèse Flames of Love: The Influence of St John of the Cross in the Life and Writings of St.Thérèse of Lisieux.* NY: Alba House, The Society of St Paul, 1999.

Habig, M. A. (ed.), *St Francis of Assisi. Writings and Early Biographies.* USA: Franciscan Herald Press, 1983.

John Paul II, Pope, *Apostolic Letter Salvifici Doloris* Rome: Vatican City, 1984.

John Paul II, Pope, *Divini Amoris Scientia,* Rome: Vatican City, 1997.

John Paul II, Pope, *Directory on Popular Piety and The Liturgy. Principles and Guidelines.* Rome: Vatican City, 2001.

John Paul II, Pope, *Ecclesia de Eucharistia.* Rome: Vatican City, 2003.

Jordan FSM, P., *An Affair of the Heart. A Biblical and Franciscan Journey.* Leominster: Gracewing, 2008.

Khanh-Nguyen-Van OFM, N., *The Teacher of His Heart. Jesus Christ in the Thought and Writings of St Francis.* Translated by E. Hagman, OFMCap New York: The Franciscan Institute, 1994.

Kinney OCD, D., *The Poetry of Saint Thérèse of Lisieux*, Washington DC: ICS Publications, 1996.

Martin, C. (Sister Genevieve of the Holy Face), *A Memoir of my Sister St Thérèse.* Dublin: M.H.Gill and Son Limited, 1959.

Matura OFM, T., *Francis of Assisi: The Message in His Writings.* Trans. By Paul Barratt, OFMCap USA: The Franciscan Institute, St Bonaventure University, 1997.

McCaffrey OCD, J., *Captive Flames: A Biblical Reading of The Carmelite Saints.* Dublin: Veritas Publications, 2005.

Monti, D. V., *Franciscans and the Scriptures: Living the Word of God.* Washington Theological Union Symposium Papers. USA: The Franciscan Institute, St Bonaventure University, 2005.

O'Mahony, C., *St Thérèse of Lisieux by those who knew her. Testimonies from the Process of Beatification.* Dublin: Veritas, 1975.

Pontifical Work for Ecclesiastical Vocations, *New Vocations for a New Europe.* Rome, 1997.

Raischl SFO, J. & Cirino OFM, A., *My Heart's Quest: Collected Writings of Eric Doyle, Friar Minor, Theologian.* Canterbury, England: Franciscan International Study Centre, 2005.

Straub, G. T., *The Sun and Moon over Assisi: A Personal Encounter with Francis and Clare.* Cincinnati, Ohio: St Anthony Messenger Press, 2000.

Synod of Bishops XI, *Lineameanta,* Rome: The Vatican, 2004.

Taylor, T. Rev, *Saint Thérèse of Lisieux: The Little Flower of Jesus.* London: Burns Oates & Washbourne Ltd., 1927.

Articles

Armstrong OFMCap, R., 'The Prophetic Implications of the Admonitions', in *Laurentianum*, vol. 26, USA: The Franciscan Institute, St Bonaventure University, 1985, pp. 396–464.

Bonaventure, Saint, 'Letter in Response to an Unknown Master'. *Works of St Bonaventure, Writings Concerning the Franciscan Order*. vol. 5, USA: The Franciscan Institute, St Bonaventure University. 1994. p. 51.

Colgan, L. M., 'The Meaning of Seraphic: Bonaventure and Francis. The Celestial Hierarch: Pseudo-Dionysius', in *The Cord*, 37/3, USA: St Bonaventure University, 1987, p. 74.

Jansen OFM, A., 'The Story of the True Joy: An Autobiographical Reading', in *Greyfriars Review*, 5/3, USA: St Bonaventure University. 1991, pp. 367–387.

Lehmann OFMCap, L. , 'We Thank You: The Structure and Content of Chapter 23 of the Earlier Rule', in *Greyfriars Review*, 5/1, USA: St Bonaventure University, 1991, pp. 1–54.

Matura OFM, T. , 'My Holy Father', in *Greyfriars Review*, 1/1, USA: St Bonaventure University, 1987, pp. 105–130.

Mico OFMCap, J., 'The Spirituality of St Francis: Minority', Translated by P. Barratt, OFMCap, in *Greyfriars Review*, 9/2, The Franciscan Institute, St Bonaventure University, 1995, pp. 125–145.

Romb, A.W., 'The Franciscan Experience of Kenosis', in *The Cord*, 41/5, USA: St Bonaventure University, 1981, pp. 145–155.

Vollot, B., 'The Diatessaron and Earlier Rule of St Francis' in *Greyfriars Review*, 6/3, USA: The Franciscan Institute, St Bonaventure University, 1992, pp. 279–317.

Lightning Source UK Ltd.
Milton Keynes UK
UKOW05f1807110814

236748UK00001B/28/P